The Workbook
on the
7 Deadly Sins

The Workbook
on the
7 Deadly Sins

Maxie Dunnam
and
Kimberly Dunnam Reisman

UPPER
ROOM BOOKS®
NASHVILLE

THE LIBRARY OF CONGRESS CATALOGING-IN-PUBLICATION DATA

Dunnam, Maxie D.
    The workbook on the seven deadly sins / by Maxie Dunnam and Kimberly Dunnam Reisman.
      p.   cm.
    Includes bibliographical references.
    ISBN 978-0-8358-0714-2 (pbk.)
    1. Deadly sins—Prayer-books and devotions—English.
    2. Devotional calendars.   3. Retreats.   I. Reisman, Kimberly Dunnam,
    1960–   . II. Title
    BV4626.D86   1997
    241' .3—dc21   97-9331
                                                 CIP

Personal Words

I receive a lot of joy from my three children: Kim, Kerry, and Kevin. It has been a special joy sharing the writing of this book with my oldest, Kim. I was ordained as a Methodist minister in 1957 and graduated from theology school in 1958. She graduated from theology school in 1991 and was ordained in 1996. There is special meaning in having a child follow in your footsteps. And it is more than special to have her walk with me in this ministry of writing.

—*Maxie D. Dunnam*

When the Lord called Samuel, the priest Eli realized what was happening before Samuel ever knew. Only after Eli told Samuel to be still and listen again did Samuel realize that it was God who was summoning him. I have had two Eli's in my life for whom I am very grateful: Buford and Jean Dickinson. Long before I was ever aware that God intended to use me, Buford and Jean encouraged me to explore my gifts and graces for God's service. Because I listened to them and then was still and listened for God, I was able to hear the call that I am striving now to follow. Buford is now part of the great cloud of witnesses that surrounds us and supports us as we seek to follow Christ. Jean remains my quiet cheerleader. I thank the Lord always for both of them.

Throughout my life I have been blessed with people like Jean and Buford, who have cheered me on as I have sought to follow God's call in my life. One in particular holds a special place and has been significant in helping me take my first baby steps in pastoral ministry: my father, Maxie Dunnam. I will always be grateful that he had faith enough in me to offer the challenge of this writing and faith in God to trust that he would provide the increase.

—*Kimberly Dunnam Reisman*

CONTENTS

INTRODUCTION

S in is real. We may be uncomfortable talking about it, but sin is a hard truth—as much a part of our lives as the air we breathe. We may try to ignore sin or pretend it's not there. We may even try to convince ourselves that the evil in our world is caused by sick people who aren't anything like us. But the truth remains: sin is real, and it's a part of each of us.

This book is about the seven deadly sins. It is offered not as a social program, or an alternative to social and governmental programs that are needed to address the ills of our day. It is offered because society is a reflection of the persons who make up that society. And all the social ills are an extension of that which seethes and rages and contorts in the hearts of individuals. While social ills must be addressed systemically, there will be no success unless the majority of the people in our communities begin to look at themselves and own the fact they are contributing, in part, to the ills that beset us.

Whether we are willing to admit it or not, all of us are engaged, to some degree or another, in an ongoing battle with sin and vice. We may not think in these terms, or even use the labels "sin" and "vice"—yet at the same time, when we look closely at ourselves, we discover misery in our life, and we see how often we give in to low passions which debase our humanity. Certainly, most of us realize that our failure to live up to our best morally results in unhappiness and causes us to realize how tragically we fall short of God's intention for us.

Paradoxically, sin, the very thing we're trying so hard to avoid, can be our summons to life! By denying our sin, however, we miss the opportunity to invigorate our lives. We miss the call to new life. When we stop taking evil seriously, when it becomes a mere coincidence of genes, or psychology, or simply someone else's fault, our ability to take good seriously begins to dwindle as well. If we aren't responsible for the bad, for sin, how is it that we're entitled to take credit for the good?

Recognizing our sinfulness, acknowledging our tendency to turn away from God, reminds us that our lives are what they are by the choices we make. What a rejuvenating idea! Taking responsibility for our sinfulness need not lead to a debilitating sense of hopelessness; rather, it opens to us the opportunity of choice. We can choose our own way, continuing to deny that our problems come from within ourselves. Or, we can choose the way of wholeness, by turning back toward the life that God has intended for us.

How we choose to deal with sin is not inconsequential. The stakes are quite high. There are benefits in choosing to turn back toward God, toward the way of wholeness: renewed connection with God in this life and the life to come; strength and guidance for our daily lives; the opportunity to tap the potential God has placed within us, to mention just a few. There are also consequences to denying our sinfulness and choosing our own way. Separation from God, and the judgment it necessitates, are the consequences of sin. God loves us unconditionally and desires to be in relationship with us. God also respects us as autonomous beings with the ability to direct our lives. Because of that great love and respect, God will always reach out for us, search for us, pull us to Godself. However, God will never violate our freedom to choose; God will never coerce us or manipulate us into being in relationship. Therefore, because our sinfulness separates us from God, because we are hopeless without God and sin makes us helpless to remedy this, the very real consequence of refusing to deal with it is continued alienation from God, not just now, but forever. This eternal separation from God should be a powerful motivator. Yet, if that possibility does not in itself lead us to address the problem of sin, it ought at least to engender within us tremendous awe for a God whose love and respect for us are so great that it refuses to compromise our integrity, even to the point of possibly losing us altogether.

The idea of listing "deadly" (capital) sins is almost as old as Christianity itself. It seems to have begun with the desert fathers in Egypt. The most concentrated attention to the idea of major or deadly sins—called this because they so greatly endangered the spiritual life—came in the fourth century. It stemmed from the flourishing monastic movement. Because the monastic life focused so intensely on the inner self and spirituality, it's not surprising that deep understanding of our sinful nature evolved there. John Cassian, a monk from Marseilles, developed a list of eight sins as a way of guiding his fellow monks. Finally, in the sixth century, Pope Gregory I (the Great) adapted the list, and reduced the number from eight to seven. This list thus became applicable not just for the monastic life but for ordinary life as well and created the list of the seven deadly sins—pride, avarice, lust, anger, gluttony, envy, and *acedia* (sloth)—that we now use.

Throughout history, at the foundation of all the discussions of the seven deadly sins is a recognition that these sins are deeply rooted in our nature. Social scientists are finally coming to the same conclusion, admitting that we are reaping the harvest of a failure to recognize the fact of sin. The early church leaders also knew that these sins do not stand alone. They are entwined together and are not limited to individuals. They knew that it's impossible to be guilty of one sin and innocent of another. They also knew that the private sins of individuals spiraled out into the community. The vices that flow from what the church has designated the seven deadly sins operate at the social level and permeate politics, commerce, entertainment—the whole of popular culture.

Pride and greed and anger certainly profoundly influence domestic and foreign policy. Standford M. Lyman in his book *The Seven Deadly Sins: Society and Evil* has provided a thoughtful analysis of how the seven deadly sins are reflected in and shape social attitudes, values, and institutions. Pornography is an outgrowth of lust; substance abuse an outgrowth of gluttony; terrorism an outgrowth of envy; violence an outgrowth of anger; indifference to the pain and suffering of others is the outgrowth of sloth; abuse of power and position of influence, public trust, is the outgrowth of greed. All sorts of things including one of the most pervasive and debilitating social ills of our day—discrimination—are the outgrowth of pride. So the seven deadly sins, while personal, certainly aren't private and have ramifications throughout society.

A second foundation of the discussion of the seven deadly sins is the understanding that they correspond with the seven cardinal virtues. As Johannes Scotus Erigena wrote in *On the*

Division of Nature, "No vice is found but is the shadow of some virtue." Wisdom, justice, temperance, and courage are four of the cardinal virtues and were taken from the Greek and Roman cultures in which the early church first found itself. These virtues were explored from the Christian perspective and given deeper meaning. The last three virtues—faith, hope, and love—are the theological virtues and have clear roots in the New Testament.

The notion for this workbook grew, in part, out of our concern for the recovery of virtue. This concern is widespread. William J. Bennett's *Book of Virtues,* published in 1995, became an overnight best-seller. We all know that something is desperately wrong in our American culture. We must somehow recover the good.

Our original intention was to deal with sin and virtue—sin to be forsaken and virtue to be cultivated. We forsook that notion almost immediately—for two reasons. One, the two subjects together were too much to deal with in one workbook. Two, and more importantly, is a theological issue. In the Christian faith we cannot deal with sin simply as a "moral" issue. The solution to sin is more radical than saying no to it or seeking to replace sin with virtue. It demands much more than our human decision and will. It requires the intervention of God and our response to God's graceful offer of Godself in Jesus Christ.

One other introductory word about sin. Throughout history, all kinds of people have struggled with and been fascinated by the dilemma of sin. We can see this interest expressed in such classic literature as "Purgatory," the second book of Dante's *The Divine Comedy;* "The Parson's Tale," from Geoffrey Chaucer's *The Canterbury Tales;* and Christopher Marlowe's *Doctor Faustus.* Even Hollywood showed its interest when it released the graphic movie *Seven.* The issue of sin and its effect on our personal lives and our larger world is as relevant now as it has been in the past. While we will seek at least to point out the connection of these seven deadly sins to our social ills, the primary purpose of this book is to focus on the individual. It is grounded in the fact of an evangelical Christian perspective that humankind is "fallen." We are sinners, by nature. Theologians often refer to this as "original sin," indicating the contention that each of us comes into the world with at least a predisposition to live in a way that separates us from our best selves, from each other, and from God. Our separation and estrangement inflict pain and suffering even upon those that we love most—and offend God, who cares for us with an unconditional love. That is the bad news. Because by nature we are sinners and are helpless to overcome evil or to succeed in saving ourselves, something miraculous has to happen. And it has happened! God has provided a way of salvation through Jesus. Jesus came to be the miracle of transformation for our human nature. His death on the cross is God's ultimate expression of love and forgiveness, which, if we accept, works that miracle of salvation in us—putting us right with God.

We will spend the first week dealing personally with a general understanding of sin and God's answer to it. We approach this fact of our nature with confidence, knowing that if we open ourselves to genuine self-exploration and to the power of the Holy Spirit to work within us through our study, God will be waiting, ready to embrace and welcome us.

We have written this book together. However, there are occasions where one of us will tell a personal story. On these occasions the pronoun "I" instead of "we" will be used. We hope that this is not confusing. Maybe you will have a bit of fun guessing who the "I" is.

The Plan

This workbook is designed for individual and group use. Let's look at the process. It is simple but very important.

I have learned from my long years of teaching and ministry with small groups that a six- to eight-week period for a group study is the most manageable and effective. Also, I have learned that persons can best appropriate content and truth in small doses. That is the reason for organizing the material in segments to be read daily.

The plan for this workbook is the same as for the previous ones I have written. It calls for an eight-week commitment. You are asked to give about thirty minutes each day to reflect on some aspect of sin and how sin expresses itself in your life. For most persons, the thirty minutes will come at the beginning of the day. If mornings are not possible, do it whenever the time is available; but do it regularly. This is not only an intellectual pursuit, though it is that, it is a spiritual journey, the purpose of which is to incorporate the content into your daily life.

It is a personal journey, but our hope is that you will share it with some fellow pilgrims who will meet together once each week during the eight weeks of the study.

The workbook is arranged into eight major divisions, each designed to guide you for one week. These divisions contain seven sections, one for each day of the week. Each day of the week will have three major aspects: reading, reflecting and recording ideas and thoughts about the material and your own understanding and experience, and some practical suggestions for incorporating ideas from the reading material into your daily life.

In each day's section, you will read something about sin and its destructive work. It won't be too much to read, but it will be enough to challenge thought and action.

Quotations from most sources other than scripture are followed by the author's name and page number on which the quote can be found. These citations are keyed to the Bibliography at the back of the workbook should you wish to read certain works more fully.

Throughout the workbook you will see this symbol ■ ■ ■ . When you come to the symbol, please stop. Do not read any further; think and reflect as you are requested to do in order to internalize the ideas being shared or the experience reflected upon.

Reflecting and Recording

After the reading each day, there will be a time for reflecting and recording. This dimension calls for you to record some of your reflections. The degree of meaning you receive from this workbook is largely dependent upon your faithfulness to its practice. You may be unable on a particular day to do precisely what is requested. If so, then simply record that fact and make a note of why you can't follow through. This may give you some insight about yourself and help you to grow.

Also, on some days there may be more suggestions than you can deal with in the time you have. Do what is most meaningful for you, and do not feel guilty.

Finally, always remember that this is a personal pilgrimage. What you write in your workbook is your private property. You may not wish to share it with anyone. For this reason, no two people should attempt to share the same workbook. The importance of what you write is not what it may mean to someone else but what it means to you. Writing, even if it is only brief notes or single-word reminders, helps us clarify our feelings and thoughts.

The significance of the reflecting and recording dimension will grow as you move along. Even beyond the eight weeks, you will find meaning in looking back to what you wrote on a particular day in response to a particular situation.

Sharing with Others

In the history of Christian spirituality, the spiritual director or spiritual guide has been a significant person. To varying degrees, most of us have had spiritual directors—persons to whom we have turned for support and direction in our spiritual pilgrimage. There is a sense in which this workbook can be a spiritual guide because you can use it as a private venture without participating in a group.

This workbook's meaning will be enhanced, however, if you share the adventure with eight to twelve others. (Larger numbers tend to limit individual involvement.) In this way, you will profit from the growing insights of others, and they will profit from yours. A guide for group sharing is included in the text at the end of each week.

If this is a group venture, all persons should begin their personal involvement with the workbook on the same day, so that when the group meets, all will have been dealing with the same material and will be at the same place in the text. An initial get-acquainted group meeting will be helpful to begin the adventure. A guide for this meeting is provided on page 14.

Group sessions are designed to last one and one-half hours (with the exception of the initial meeting). Group members should covenant to attend all sessions unless an emergency prevents attendance. There will be eight weekly sessions in addition to this first get-acquainted time.

Group Leader's Tasks

One person may provide the leadership or leaders may be assigned from week to week. The leader's tasks are to:

1. Read the directions and determine ahead of time how to handle the session. It may not be possible to use all the suggestions for sharing and praying together. Feel free to select those you think will be most meaningful and those for which you have adequate time.
2. Model a style of openness, honesty, and warmth. A leader should not ask anyone to share what he or she is not willing to share. Usually, the leader should be the first to share, especially as it relates to personal experiences.
3. Moderate the discussion.
4. Encourage reluctant members to participate and try to prevent a few persons from doing all the talking.
5. Keep the sharing centered in personal experience rather than academic debate.
6. Honor the time schedule. If it appears necessary to go longer than one and one-half hours, the leader should get consensus for continuing another twenty or thirty minutes.
7. See that the meeting time and place are known by all, especially if meetings are held in different homes.

8. Make sure that the necessary materials for meetings are available and that the meeting room is arranged ahead of time.

It is a good idea for weekly meetings to be held in the homes of the participants. (Hosts or hostesses should make sure there are as few interruptions as possible from children, telephones, pets, and so forth.) If the meetings are held in a church, they should be in an informal setting. Participants are asked to dress casually, to be comfortable and relaxed.

If refreshments are served, they should come *after* the formal meeting. In this way, those who wish to stay longer for informal discussion may do so, while those who need to keep to the time schedule will be free to leave but will get the full value of the meeting time.

Suggestions for Initial Get-Acquainted Meeting

Since the initial meeting is for the purpose of getting acquainted and beginning the shared pilgrimage, here is a way to get started.

1. Have each person in the group give his or her full name and the name by which each wishes to be called. Address all persons by the first name or nickname. If name tags are needed, provide them. Each person should make a list of the names somewhere in his or her workbook.
2. Let each person in the group share one of the happiest, most exciting, or most meaningful experiences he or she has had during the past three or four weeks.
3. After this experience of happy sharing, ask each person who is willing to share his or her expectations of this workbook study. Why did he or she become a part of it? What does each expect to gain from it? What are the reservations?
4. The leader should now review the introduction to the workbook and ask if there are questions about directions and procedures. (The leader should have read the introduction prior to the meeting.) If persons have not received copies of the workbook, the books should be handed out now. Remember that every person must have his or her own workbook.
5. Day 1 in the workbook is the day following this initial meeting, and the next meeting should be held on Day 7 of the first week. If the group must choose a weekly meeting time other than seven days from this initial session, the reading assignment should be adjusted so that the weekly meetings are always on Day 7, and Day 1 is always the day following a weekly meeting.
6. Nothing binds group members together more than praying for one another. The leader should encourage each participant to write the names of all persons in the group in his or her workbook and commit to praying for them by name daily during the seven weeks.
7. After checking to see that everyone knows the time and place of the next meeting, the leader should close with a prayer, thanking God for each person in the group and for the opportunity for growth.

Week One

Taking Sin Seriously

DAY 1

Our Common Story

Now the serpent was more crafty than any other wild animal that the LORD God had made. He said to the woman, "Did God say, 'You shall not eat from any tree in the garden'?" The woman said to the serpent, "We may eat of the fruit of the trees in the garden; but God said, 'You shall not eat of the fruit of the tree that is in the middle of the garden, nor shall you touch it, or you shall die.'" But the serpent said to the woman, "You will not die; for God knows that when you eat of it your eyes will be opened, and you will be like God, knowing good and evil." So when the woman saw that the tree was good for food, and that it was a delight to the eyes, and that the tree was to be desired to make one wise, she took of its fruit and ate; and she also gave some to her husband, who was with her, and he ate. Then the eyes of both were opened, and they knew that they were naked; and they sewed fig leaves together and made loincloths for themselves.

—Genesis 3:1-7

One of the best and most exciting ways to study history is to read biography. Likewise, one of the most rich and rewarding ways to study scripture is to focus on persons—persons through whom God exercised divine providential care, spoke a powerful word, and expressed God's will.

The drama of humankind moves through two people: Adam and Eve. In creating them, God freely chooses to bind Godself to them and all creation and produces a gracious relationship of love that is always growing. They are made in the image of God; they are sinless and are placed in a situation unmarred by evil. The stage is set for conflict as Adam and Eve eat the forbidden fruit, suddenly become aware of their nakedness and guilt, seek to hide only to be confronted by God, and then are driven from Paradise. We have called this drama "The Fall."

Whatever else we get from the story, this much is clear. We're not only creatures of God, we're creatures in rebellion against our Creator. We are living in a situation of separation from God, without the peace and harmony envisioned by God at Creation. When we understand and accept this, the story of Adam and Eve, the serpent and the garden, becomes the story of every person. It's your story, my story. Adam and Eve are you and me.

Consider the movement of this common story. First, we are *gardeners*. In our innocence, we are in harmony with God, with the community around us, with our fellows. Then we become *rebels*. We won't accept our humanity. We want to be as God. We eat the forbidden fruit and life is never the same again. The result is that we become *fugitives*, plagued by guilt, hiding from God.

Interpret the Fall how you will, and there is much more to it than most of us have been willing to face, yet the obvious fact is there: this is my experience, your experience.

Dramatized in this Garden of Eden story is the truth that humankind, made to go God's way, has the besetting tendency to take our own way. It is in this sense that Adam and Eve are every person—their experience is the universal experience. There is something in us that impels us to put ourselves and our interests first. Deep within, sometimes so subtly that we can't identify it, the purpose emerges—to be independent of God, to be the master of our fate and the captain of our soul. None of us lives very long before we begin to put ourselves where God should be—at the center of our world. We don't live too long before we begin to assert our independence and sovereignty, before we begin to live as though we were adequate within ourselves.

We were created in God's image, whole, but sin entered the picture. Adam and Eve were beguiled by the serpent, and they chose their way against God's will. So we marred the image, perverted the wholeness, rebelled, and became fugitives, not only from God but from God's true intention for our life. The struggle of our life is an inner and an outer one, as we wander endlessly in the land "east of Eden." That's the drama that describes our predicament, our common story.

Reflecting and Recording

The movement of the Eden story is revealing. The temptation to disobedience comes from without—in the form of a serpent. Most of us know the inner urges—those passions that take over our wills to cause us to act in destructive, sinful ways. But here in the beginning, the first temptation to disobedience comes from without. Spend a few minutes reflecting on the sin nature as "alien"—that this is not God's intention for us.

■ ■ ■

The sinuous gliding of the snake is a picture of the slyness in the suggestion of sin. The forbidden fruit is not dangled before Eve. There is the planting of doubt about God's prohibition: "Did God say . . . ?" Reflect on how something works in our minds to question whether what we are considering has anything to do with our relationship to God.

■ ■ ■

The snake distorts what the fruit is all about, implying that God is not saving us from an abyss of darkness and destruction, but preventing us from rising to a higher plane: "You will not die; for God knows that when you eat of it your eyes will be opened, and you will be like God, knowing good and evil" (Gen. 3:4-5). By shrewdly manipulating the consequences, the serpent casts doubt on God's motives, slyly shifting God from a divine protector to an almighty hindrance.

Reflect on the way sin gets at us—how we give in to the lies that seduce us: (1) It will do you no harm; (2) You're cheating yourself of pleasure and good by not doing it.

■ ■ ■

During the Day

It helps us in ordering our life and keeping perspective to have at least one thing that we are committed to do, or one touchstone of truth which we will call to mind, or some direction for assessing our attitude. Test the dynamic today by using this question: "Where is the serpent in this?" When a feeling or uncertainty arises about what you should say, how you should act, what you are feeling, pause and ask, *"Where is the serpent in this?" Am I being tempted? Is there the possibility of deceit?*

DAY 2

Whatever Happened to Sin?

One of the best books we read in our research for writing this workbook was *The Seven Deadly Sins Today* by Henry Fairlie. Fairlie, who describes himself as a reluctant believer, explains in his preface why he chose to write on this subject:

> I have for a long time thought that the psychological explanations of the waywardness of our own behavior and the sociological explanations of the evils of our societies have come very nearly to a dead end. They have taken us so far, but not very far, and it is hard to see, in whatever direction they may move, that they will take us much farther. They have come to this impasse because they shirk the problem of evil, and they shirk it because of the major premise on which they rest: that our own faults and those of our societies are the result of some kind of mechanical failure, which has only to be diagnosed and understood for us to set it right. Yet none of the schemes for improvement, personal or social, have made much difference, and some would even say that they have made things worse.
>
> —Fairlie, p. vii

So here is an unbeliever, albeit *reluctant*, writing a book about sin—and one of the best books that we have read.

In the early 1970s the psychiatrist Karl Menninger's challenging book *Whatever Became of Sin?* was first published. His plea was that we not write off all the unpleasant behavior of humankind as maladjustment or reduce evil to a legal problem by calling it crime.

Augustine of Hippo is one of the premier theologians of all time. In his classic book *Confessions*, he told the story of his youthful escapade of stealing pears from a neighbor's tree. He recorded that late one night a group of youngsters went to shake down and rob the tree. They took a great quantity of fruit from it, "not to eat them ourselves, but simply to throw them to the pigs." He went on to berate himself for the depth of sin this act revealed: "It was only my love of mischief that made me do it. The evil in me was foul, but I loved it. . . . My soul was vicious and broke away from your safe keeping to seek its own destruction."

One might ask, Why would a harmless prank such as this loom so large in the mind of this great theologian? By his own admission, he had taken a mistress, fathered a child out of wedlock, and indulged in every fleshly passion. Surely, any of these was more serious than stealing pears.

But Augustine saw in the "pear incident" his true nature and the nature of all humankind: in each of us there is sin. Likewise, a psychiatrist would write a book *Whatever Happened to Sin?* and a best-selling author who describes himself as a reluctant unbeliever would give attention to the seven deadly sins—all because of the fact that sin is universal. Whether we reckon with it or not, it will reckon with us. Sin is deadly and destructive—destructive of our relationship with God, relationship with those we love, and certainly destructive of the inner harmony and peace that we all long for.

Look at more of the garden of Eden story, which we began to read yesterday:

They heard the sound of the LORD God walking in the garden at the time of the evening breeze, and the man and his wife hid themselves from the presence of the LORD God among the trees of the garden. But the LORD God called to the man, and said to him, "Where are you?" He said, "I heard the sound of you in the garden, and I was afraid, because I was naked; and I hid myself." He said, "Who told you that you were naked? Have you eaten from the tree of which I commanded you not to eat?" The man said, "The woman whom you gave to be with me, she gave me fruit from the tree, and I ate." Then the LORD God said to the woman, "What is this that you have done?" The woman said, "The serpent tricked me, and I ate."

Then the LORD God said, "See, the man has become like one of us, knowing good and evil; and now, he might reach out his hand and take also from the tree of life, and eat, and live forever"—therefore the LORD God sent him forth from the garden of Eden, to till the ground from which he was taken. He drove out the man; and at the east of the garden of Eden he placed the cherubim, and a sword flaming and turning to guard the way to the tree of life.

—Genesis 3:8-13, 22-24

It's a dramatic picture and, as we suggested yesterday, it is our common story.

Reflecting and Recording

Continue reflecting on the movement of the Eden story. When they ate the forbidden fruit, Adam and Eve did not become "like gods" as the tempter had promised. Rather, their "ignorant innocence" changed to "bitter knowledge." Their nakedness became a matter of shame and they sought to cover themselves. More seriously yet, their relationship with God was broken. They now knew guilt and they sought to hide from God. Spend a few minutes reflecting on this assertion: *Man and woman had an Eden and lost it.*

■ ■ ■

Can you locate in your own experience something like Augustine's pear incident that says, "Yes, in each of us there is sin"? Describe that experience briefly.

Spend a few minutes now reflecting on this assertion: *Since the fall of Adam and Eve, the whole human race is sinful by nature.* What does it mean? Do you believe it? Is it confirmed in your own life?

■ ■ ■

During the Day

Continue to use the question, *Where is the serpent in this?* as a direction for assessing your attitude and action.

DAY 3

Sin: The Act of a Traitor

Have mercy on me, O God, according to your steadfast love; according to your abundant mercy blot out my transgressions. Wash me thoroughly from my iniquity, and cleanse me from my sin. For I know my transgressions, and my sin is ever before me. Against you, you alone, have I sinned, and done what is evil in your sight, so that you are justified in your sentence and blameless when you pass judgment. Indeed, I was born guilty, a sinner when my mother conceived me. You desire truth in the inward being; therefore teach me wisdom in my secret heart.

—Psalm 51:1-6

Sin is more like the act of a traitor than that of a criminal. A criminal breaks the law of his country; a traitor betrays his country. A criminal violates the law; a traitor violates his citizenship, his identity, his trust. This is what the psalmist is saying: "Against you, you alone, have I sinned" (v. 4).

This psalm is most often ascribed to David and is set in the context of his sin with Bathsheba (2 Sam. 11–12). Recall the story. From his rooftop, David saw Bathsheba bathing, and lust raged within. We usually think of adultery; rape was involved also. David *ordered* Bathsheba brought to him so he might satisfy his burning sexual lust. David was the king, so Bathsheba had no choice in the matter. David's rape and adultery led to deception—and deception to murder. Bathsheba conceived. In order to cover his sin, David dug the pit deeper by having her husband, Uriah, a military leader, sent into the front lines of battle to be killed. So, David is guilty of a whole chain of sins.

The Lord confronted David through Nathan, the prophet, with the ringing words, "You are the man!" (2 Sam. 12:7). This brought David to his knees before God. The child conceived from his sin with Bathsheba died. David, broken in spirit, contrite in heart, pled for mercy. When he confessed to Nathan, "I have sinned against the LORD," Nathan replied, "Now the LORD has put away your sin; you shall not die" (2 Sam. 12:13). It is out of all of this that Psalm 51 comes: David's deep, prayerful, agonizing response to his catastrophe.

David uses three words to express his treason against God: *transgressions*, *iniquity*, and *sin*. Looking at the entire psalm, you see the reiteration of confession and pleading, usually in a threefold pattern. This is typical of Hebrew poetry, called parallelism. But Alexander Maclaren in *Expositions of the Holy Scripture* reminds us that "this is not a mere piece of Hebrew parallelism. . . . It is much more the earnestness of a soul that cannot be content with once asking for the blessings and then passing on, but dwells upon them with repeated supplication, not because it thinks that it shall be heard for its 'much speaking,' but because it longs for them so eagerly. . . . Though the three clauses do express the same general idea, they express it under various modifications, and must be all taken together before we get the whole of the psalmist's thought of sin." (Maclaren, p. 145)

The three words the psalmist employs, therefore, give prominence to different aspects of sin. "'Transgression' is not the same as 'iniquity,' and 'iniquity' is not the same as 'sin.' They are not aimless, useless synonyms, but they have each a separate thought in them." (Maclaren, p. 4) *Transgression* literally means "rebellion"; iniquity literally means that "which is twisted or bent"; and the original word for sin literally means "missing a mark or an aim."

The word *transgression* (rebellion) is the one that suggests treason and best indicates why David says with passionate penitence, "Against you, you alone, have I sinned" (Ps. 51:4). He expresses a touching sense of helplessness in verse 5: "Indeed, I was born guilty, a sinner when my mother conceived me." David is expressing the reality of sin's pervasiveness. Sin's infection is present in us all. When the infection is pervasive enough to determine our attitude and action, we become "traitors" to God.

Reflecting and Recording

Since Adam's fall, the whole human race is sinful by nature. It's one thing to affirm this truth intellectually; it's quite another to own it as a reality shaping your life. A powerful aspect of sin is denial. We'll deal with this more on Day 5. For now, simply register this fact: It is not fatal to be a sinner; denying that you are a sinner is fatal.

To further the process of acknowledging sin, to begin to break out of denial, consider again the nature of sin as revealed in Psalm 51:

Transgression—rebellion
Iniquity—twisted or bent
Sin—missing a mark or an aim.

Look at your life as a whole. Write a paragraph, using the three words to describe stages of your life in relation to God, others, and your "best self."

What was the last sin you committed? Write a sentence to make it specific.

Now look at each of the aspects of sin listed above. Which aspect most nearly describes the sin you just named?

■ ■ ■

If you have not yet specifically confessed to God the sin you named above, take a time of prayer now, verbalize your confession, ask and receive God's forgiveness.

■ ■ ■

During the Day

Plant these words solidly in your mind: *transgression, iniquity, missing the mark*. Stay aware of them as you continue to ask, *Where is the serpent in this?*

DAY 4

Original Sin

Theologians talk about "original sin." Some define this as a distortion of the image of God within us, or as an absence of something originally there at Creation. Both lead to a susceptibility to sin. Anthony Campolo states it more strongly: "Each of us comes into the world with a predisposition to live in such a way as to inflict pain on those who love us most, and to offend the God who cares for us infinitely." (*Seven Deadly Sins*, p. 9)

The understanding of sin's destructive place in our life swings between total depravity and extreme distortion. In the extreme notion of total depravity, the person is absolutely helpless to act in any way contributing to her salvation. From a less extreme perspective, others contend that though original sin has virtually obliterated what God had intended humanity to be, a small shred of the *imago Dei* (image of God) remains in us. This extremely distorted, but still residual, God-print upon us is sufficient to resonate with God's initiative toward us, drawing us into God's gracious redemption.

One way of seeing the difference is the use of a slang expression: Is it total or *tee-total* depravity? Our perspective is that of depravity but not tee-total depravity. There is within us that residual God-print that Augustine said "keeps us restless" until we rest in God.

This is the way Paul experienced it and expressed it:

> I know that nothing good dwells within me, that is, in my flesh. I can will what is right, but I cannot do it. For I do not do the good I want, but the evil I do not want is what I do. Now if I do what I do not want, it is no longer I that do it, but sin that dwells within me. So I find it to be a law that when I want to do what is good, evil lies close at hand. For I delight in the law of God in my inmost self, but I see in my members another law at war with the law of my mind, making me captive to the law of sin that dwells in my members. Wretched man that I am! Who will rescue me from this body of death? Thanks be to God through Jesus Christ our Lord!
>
> —Romans 7:18-25

However we talk about it, sooner or later morally and spiritually sensitive persons discover that not just a proneness to sin but sin as a reality, a power, is a part of our life. Paul's word, quoted above, is not an isolated word in the Bible. It is the witness of the whole of scripture poured out by Paul in a personal confession. Is there a more touching expression of a raging civil war within? "I know that nothing good dwells within me, that is, in my flesh. I can will what is right, but I cannot do it. . . . Wretched man that I am! Who will rescue me from this body of death?" (Rom. 7:18, 24). What a raging fire of conscience! What a gripping heart cry! How often do we feel that ripping inside, the tearing apart of our efforts to be whole and centered and headed in a clear direction?

How can we be naive about sin in our life? Yet, there are those who still think it impertinent and impulsive to talk about sin. For them, the problems of society and personal misery are located not in our alienation from God—not in our sin—but somewhere else. Our ignorance, not our sin, is the problem. Psychological maladjustment, not sin, is our dilemma. Our surroundings are what "get to us"—not sin. Our feelings of powerlessness—not our sin is the reason we're so impotent in living effectively in the world. Economic inequities, limited education, inequality among persons—not sin—are driving our society to madness and violence. So, if we improve education, if we cultivate self-understanding, if we come to a point of self-actualization, if everybody's standard of living is raised above the poverty level, if we arrange proper socialization for everyone, then people will be saved and will be happy and fulfilled. Social evil will disappear, and the problems of the world will be solved.

But the witness of history, especially contemporary history, reveals the lie in these assumptions. With the full flowering of the eighteenth century, the pinnacles reached in education, science, technology, and secular human development, we still had the Holocaust. Before and during World War II an estimated six million Jews were killed. And there is the less well-known killing of Christians estimated at fifteen million by Lenin and Stalin in a secular, materialistic, godless vision of society.

Sin is at the heart of our lives and penetrates to the core. If it is not expressed in the moment, it is there, just beneath the surface, ready to break out in attitudes and actions that will be destructive. That's what we mean when we talk about original sin. In a sense, there's nothing original about it, because we're all infected by it.

Reflecting and Recording

Write a paragraph in response to this statement: We sin because we are sinners.

Yesterday, we considered three aspects of sin: transgression, iniquity, and missing the mark. The Old Testament word translated iniquity literally means "twisted" or "bent." Is that the way you described or defined iniquity in your reflection yesterday?

■ ■ ■

Compare your thoughts about transgression and iniquity. Which seems the more awful or destructive as you commonly give meaning to those words?

■ ■ ■

Close your time, praying the Lord's Prayer. (Note: While praying the Lord's Prayer, instead of saying "Forgive us our debts," pray "Forgive us our trespasses, as we forgive those who trespass against us.")

During the Day

The word you used for sin in the Lord's Prayer is *trespasses*: "Forgive us our trespasses as we forgive those who trespass against us." Some forms of the prayer render it, "Forgive us our debts." Today, keep the word *trespass* in your mind. See if this will make you sensitive to the presence of sin—or to the temptation to sin.

DAY 5

Sin Is Denial

Go and proclaim in the hearing of Jerusalem, Thus says the LORD: I remember the devotion of your youth, your love as a bride, how you followed me in the wilderness, in a land not sown. Israel was holy to the LORD, the first fruits of his harvest. All who ate of it were held guilty; disaster came upon them, says the LORD. Hear the word of the LORD, O house of Jacob, and all the families of the house of Israel. Thus says the LORD: What wrong did your ancestors find in me that they went far from me, and went after worthless things, and became worthless themselves? They did not say, "Where is the LORD who brought us up from the land of Egypt, who led us in the wilderness, in a land of deserts and pits, in a land of drought and deep darkness, in a land that no one passes through, where no one lives?" I brought you into a plentiful land to eat its fruits and its good things. But when you entered you defiled my land, and made my heritage an abomination. The priests did not say, "Where is the LORD?" Those who handle the law did not know me; the rulers transgressed against me; the prophets prophesied by Baal, and went after things that do not profit. Therefore, once more I accuse you, says the LORD, and I accuse your children's children. Cross to the coasts of Cyprus and look, send to Kedar and examine with care; see if there has ever been such a thing. Has a nation changed its gods, even though they are no gods? But my people have changed their glory for something that does not profit. Be appalled, O heavens, at this, be shocked, be utterly desolate, says the LORD, for my people have committed two evils: they have forsaken me, the fountain of living water, and dug out cisterns for themselves, cracked cisterns that can hold no water.

—Jeremiah 2:2-13

Jeremiah was one of the last prophets that God sent to Judah before that nation and culture collapsed completely. Judah was invaded and the people carried away into Babylonian exile. The book of Jeremiah is God's word to the people through the prophet Jeremiah. The above passage is a part of the first of a series of confronting and challenging sermons that Jeremiah preaches—trying to show all the people of Judah why their life is falling apart, why their culture is crumbling, and why their family structures are collapsing.

The people of Israel were asking, "What is wrong with us? Why are things falling apart? Why are we suffering? What has gone wrong?" Through Jeremiah, God answers them. Sin. Verse 13: "My people have committed two evils: they have forsaken me, the fountain of living water, and dug out cisterns for themselves, cracked cisterns that can hold no water."

But the people of Judah could not admit that they had forsaken the Lord; they could not own the fact that they had followed "worthless idols" (Jer. 2:8, 11, NIV). Isn't that always the case?

The essence of sin is denial. Dr. Timothy Keller, pastor of Redeemer Presbyterian Church in New York City, reminds us that Jeremiah's message is intervention language.

A friend you have known for years has been hiding something. Finally, the destructive behavior that she thought she was hiding has come out and is obvious. But she still won't see it, won't accept it. She calls you in desperation. You go over. You sit down. You hear her story. She doesn't admit it, so you try to put it into perspective. "Can't you see what you're doing to yourself? You're killing yourself. Can't you see it? Don't you see the source of the bitterness in your life?" You confront the person and, if need be, you engage others to join you in the intervention. This is what Jeremiah is doing—seeking to shock Judah out of her denial.

Alcoholism is among the most familiar contemporary experiences of denial. The powerful evil of alcoholism is that it puts out a force field of denial. The alcoholic never comes to grips with his disease nor will he ever be successful in his struggle with alcohol until he becomes honest. Alcoholism is a deadly disease, but it is not fatal to be an alcoholic. It is fatal to deny that you are an alcoholic.

We come back to the consideration we began in our Reflecting and Recording on Day 3: *It is not fatal to be a sinner; denying that you are a sinner is fatal.* This is the reason this workbook journey is so important. The sins with which we are going to deal are not called *deadly* for naught. If unrecognized and not dealt with, they will destroy us. Certainly they will bring interior dislocation of the soul, which will make us dysfunctional as persons, rob us of meaning, prevent wholeness in relationships, and keep us estranged from God.

Most of us never see the magnitude of our sins. This is because the essence of sin is denial. Part of the process of this study is recognition—facing up to the way the deadly sins are expressed in our lives, confessing and repenting of those sins, receiving power for overcoming, and finding resources to engage the ongoing battle which, to some degree, we will always have to wage.

Reflecting and Recording

To begin the process of recognition, here is a listing of the seven deadly sins. Move slowly through the list and put a check over those you most readily recognize in your life.

   pride   sloth   envy   anger   greed/avarice   gluttony   lust

Now write a few sentences describing how each of the sins you checked is expressed in you.

Spend as much time as you have left reflecting on this assertion: *It is not fatal to be a sinner; denying that you are a sinner is fatal.*

During the Day

As you move through the day, be alert to how the sins you have identified find expression in your thought and behavior.

DAY 6

Sin: Personal and Social, Real and Powerful

Martin Luther said that human nature is so corrupt and blind that it does not see or sense the greatness of sin. Charles Schultz, who was almost as much a theologian as he was a cartoonist, makes the same case quite differently. In one of the Lucy and Charlie Brown confrontations, Lucy offers Charlie Brown a diagnosis of his problem. When Lucy sees that he doesn't want to listen to her, she shouts, "The whole trouble with you is you won't listen to what the whole trouble with you is!" (*The Gospel According to Peanuts*, p. 35) Jesus speaks to the issue in Mark 7:14-15, 21-22:

> Then he called the crowd again and said to them, "Listen to me, all of you, and understand: there is nothing outside a person that by going in can defile, but the things that come out are what defile. . . . For it is from within, from the human heart, that evil intentions come: fornication, theft, murder, adultery, avarice, wickedness, deceit, licentiousness, envy, slander, pride, folly."

Jesus is not saying that there is no presence of sin or evil outside us, exerting power and influence. Rather, he is suggesting that the "seat" of sin is inside us. We decide whether to let sin influence and/or control us.

On Day 1, we made the case that *sin is real*. This truth is underscored in the first chapter of the Bible. The rebellion of Adam and Eve; Cain's murder of his brother, Abel; the injustice and even barbarity of kings and other leaders; and the obscene plundering of God's creation are dramatic depictions of the destructive reality of sin. It's all there in the Bible, the most realistic book in the world regarding human nature.

Along with insisting that sin is real, the Bible also makes the case that sin is personal. That's what Jesus is saying in the passage above, and that's what Lucy was screaming at Charlie Brown. But sin is also social. While sin begins in the human heart, it flows out to poison and destroy relationships. It even becomes embedded in social customs, institutions, and structures. Immediate expressions of systemic sin come to mind. Slavery was eradicated by law, but the sin of it continued in expressions of racism, such as laws which disallowed African-Americans voting rights and relegated them to inferior schools.

The Nazi engineering of the Holocaust and the promulgation of apartheid in the Republic of South Africa are dramatic examples of sin expressing itself in unjust social structures and ideologies. Add to these the racism and sexism that presently plague our nation and you have expressions of social sin which the New Testament calls "principalities and powers." What begins *inside* us goes public in historical, social, and political sin. Now *outside* us, like a boomerang, it returns to act on us.

To fail to recognize the power of sin is, as we considered yesterday, to be in denial. In the New Testament the strength and destructive power of sin is witnessed to in terms of "demon possession."

New Testament readers will remember the story of Legion, who lived in a cemetery cut off from life, turned in on himself in destructive behavior, often bound in chains because the demon possession controlled him. (See Luke 8:26-39.) And the story of Mary Magdalene, whom Jesus freed from seven demons. (See Luke 8:2.) Whatever else we learn from these stories and the image of demon possession, this lesson is paramount: Sin is strong and it is more than an attitude or action; it is a power that can control us. We may give in to pride, lust, greed, anger, gluttony, envy and sloth, until we no longer have control—sin controls us.

Reflecting and Recording

Look at your community. Are there any expressions of power, political life, social systems where signs of the power of sin are evident? Make some notes about this: What is happening? Who is suffering? Who is in control? How did the condition come about?

Look now at your "community sins" as you have recorded them. Which of the seven deadly sins are operating to bring about these conditions? List them here.

Yesterday you were asked to identify any of the seven deadly sins most readily recognizable in your life. Look at the list again. Is there any connection between the sins you recognize in your life and what you see in your community? Spend a few minutes thinking about this.

■ ■ ■

During the Day

Henry Fairlie says, "We can recognize evil in others, but if we wish to look on the face of sin, we will see it most clearly in ourselves" (p. 17). Keep this word in mind as you move through the day. When you observe anything that hints at sin and evil in another, let that be a call to look at your own life and examine the forces operating there.

DAY 7

The Remedy for Our Sin

There is a vast difference between the last verses of Romans 7 and the first verse of Romans 8. Look at the last words from chapter 7.

> I do not understand my own actions. For I do not do what I want, but I do the very thing I hate. Now if I do what I do not want, I agree that the law is good. But in fact it is no longer I that do it, but sin that dwells within me. For I know that nothing good dwells within me, that is, in my flesh. I can will what is right, but I cannot do it. For I do not do the good I want, but the evil I do not want is what I do. Now if I do what I do not want, it is no longer I that do it, but sin that dwells within me.
>
> —Romans 7:15-20

Paul goes on to say that the struggle that is going on in his soul is really a civil war—and he is being brought under captivity to the law of sin. He groans and moans: "Wretched man that I am!" (Rom. 7:24). And then he raises that anguished question: "Who will rescue me from this body of death?" He answers that question immediately: "Thanks be to God through Jesus Christ our Lord!" Paul opens Romans 8 with this glorious word: "There is therefore now no condemnation for those who are in Christ Jesus . . . who walk not according to the flesh but according to the Spirit" (vv. 1, 4).

Do you see the tremendous difference between Paul's condition which he expresses so dramatically in chapter 7—"Wretched man that I am!" and the beginning of chapter 8—"There is therefore now no condemnation for those who are in Christ Jesus"?

One way of understanding this process is this: Justification is what God does *for* us; sanctification is what God does *in* us. So, we are not "saved" apart from justification. There is no salvation without justification; but justification does not exhaust the work of Christ on the cross or the meaning of salvation.

To put it simply, the grace of Christ comes to us in at least two forms: pardon and power. As pardon (justification), grace forgives our sins, nullifies our guilt, and heals our relationship with God from whom we are estranged because of our sin. As power, grace delivers us from our slavery to sin, the grip of sin on our lives, and fills us with the power of new life—a life in which Christ lives in us and we live through him. We can't give our sins to Jesus (if we could do that, we would all be sin-free saints)—we give ourselves to Jesus, and he takes our sins from us and gives us the power to overcome sin's grip.

The power form of grace takes us back to the theological idea of original sin discussed on Day 4. While many believe that the image of God within us is so distorted that it is impossible for us to participate at all in our salvation by God, we believe that there is enough of that image left to at least flicker in a response to God's initiative. Thinking in these terms allows us to see the power of God's grace awakening something deep within us which then responds. Here we can see the working of the Holy Spirit in our lives. As we grow in faith, as grace moves us to accept more and more readily the opportunity for new life, the Holy Spirit sustains us with the power we need to persevere and mature. The transformation of our sinful selves is not a magical change that happens overnight; rather, it is a gradual working of the Spirit on our lives, a process which requires our active and committed participation. When we are moved to accept God's grace through Christ in the form of pardon, we then begin the adventure of sanctification—the experience of empowerment by the Holy Spirit which works on our wills, giving us the strength we need to continue moving toward the wholeness God has intended for us all along.

That is the aim of this workbook journey. We will examine ourselves in relation to the seven deadly sins. As we find expressions of these sins in our life, we will not wallow in shame and guilt. We will claim our justification—gracious forgiveness and pardon of God. But we will not stop there. We will yield our lives to Christ—with special attention to that area of our lives where sin is expressing itself. We will invite Christ to take that sin from us. We will claim the power of the Holy Spirit to give us the desire and the strength of will to overcome sin's grip. We will practice disciplines that free us and even protect us from willful sin.

Reflecting and Recording

Spend some time thinking about salvation as we have presented it. You may want to read this whole section again. Is there any new insight? Is this the way you have thought about it? How have you perceived your own salvation? Make some notes in response to these questions as you examine where you are right now in your salvation journey.

Close your time in prayer now, making whatever commitment you need to make to Christ.

During the Day

If you are a part of a group using this workbook, your weekly meeting will be today. Make your plans to attend because this is an important part of your journey. Call one person in the group to touch base, and tell him or her how you look forward to this time of sharing. Don't hesitate to be honest—expressing fear or reservations or some difficult time you may have had this week. This will strengthen the fellowship and encourage the kind of openness that is essential for the group to be effective.

Also, look at the "guide for sharing" on the following pages, and make whatever preparation is necessary.

Group Meeting for Week One

Introduction

These group sessions will be most meaningful as they reflect the experience of all the participants. This guide is simply an effort to facilitate personal sharing. Therefore, do not be rigid in following these suggestions. The leader, especially, should seek to be sensitive to what is going on in the lives of the participants and to focus the group's sharing on those experiences. Ideas are important. We should wrestle with new ideas as well as with ideas with which we disagree. It is important, however, that the group meeting not become a debate about ideas. The emphasis should be on persons—experiences, feelings, and meaning. Content is important—but how content applies to our individual lives, our relationship to God and others, is most important.

As the group comes to the place where all can share honestly and openly what is happening in their lives, the more meaningful the experience will be. This does not mean sharing only the good or positive; share also the struggles, the difficulties, the negatives.

This process is not easy; it is deceptive to pretend it is. Growth requires effort. Don't be afraid to share your questions, reservations, and "dry periods," as well as that in which you find meaning.

Sharing Together

1. You may begin your time together by allowing time for each person in the group to share his or her most meaningful day with the workbook this week. The leader should begin this sharing. Tell why that particular day was so meaningful.
2. Now share your most difficult day. Tell what you experienced and why it was so difficult.
3. On Day 1 you were asked to reflect on the way sin gets at us: (1) It will do you no harm; 2) you are cheating yourself of pleasure and good by not doing it. Spend four or five minutes, allowing persons to respond generally to these ideas.
4. Invite two or three persons to share their "pear" experience which says, "Yes, in each of us, there is sin." (Refer to Day 2.)
5. Spend five to ten minutes discussing the following two statements. (1) We are not sinners because we sin; we sin because we are sinners; and (2) It is not fatal to be a sinner; denying you are a sinner is fatal.
6. Spend the balance of your time discussing the social dimensions of sin and designating expressions of it in your community.

Praying Together

Each week the group is asked to pray together. Corporate prayer is one of the great blessings of Christian community. There is power in corporate prayer, and it is important that this dimension be included in our shared pilgrimage.

It is also important that you feel comfortable in this and that no pressure be placed on anyone to pray aloud. Silent corporate prayer may be as vital and meaningful as verbal corporate prayer.

God does not need to hear our words spoken aloud to hear our prayers. Silence, where thinking is centered and attention is focused, may provide our deepest periods of prayer. There is power, however, in a community on a common journey verbalizing their thoughts and feelings to God in the presence of their fellow pilgrims.

Verbal prayers should be offered spontaneously as a person chooses to pray aloud—not "let's go around the circle now, and each one pray."

Suggestions for this "praying together" time will be given each week. The leader for the week should regard these only as suggestions. What is happening in the meeting—the mood, the needs that are expressed, the timing—should determine the direction of the group praying together. Here are some possibilities for this closing period.

1. Let the group think back over the sharing that has taken place during this session. What personal needs or concerns came out of the sharing? Begin to speak these aloud—any person verbalizing a need or a concern that has been expressed. Don't hesitate to mention a concern that you may have picked up from another; for example, "Mary isn't able to be with us this week because her son is in the hospital. Let's pray for her son and for her."

    It will be helpful for each person to make notes of the concerns and needs that are mentioned. Enter deliberately into a period of silence. Let the leader verbalize each of these needs successively, allowing for a brief period following each so that persons in the group may center their attention and focus their prayers on the person, need, or concern mentioned. All of this will be in silence as each person prays in his or her own way.

2. Invite any two persons to offer a spontaneous brief verbal prayer.

    One, thanking God for the group and the opportunity to share with others in this study/learning/prayer experience. Two, confessing that we are all sinners in need of God's love and forgiveness, asking God to open each of us to ourselves and to each other, to be honest in our sharing and genuine care for each other, and to be open to receive truth as it comes from God.

    The following is a prayer of confession from a Service of Holy Communion. (*The United Methodist Hymnal*, p. 8) Let the group pray together in closing:

Merciful God,
we confess that we have not loved you with our whole heart.
We have failed to be an obedient church.
We have not done your will,
we have broken your law,

we have rebelled against your love,
we have not loved our neighbors,
and we have not heard the cry of the needy.
Forgive us, we pray.
Free us for joyful obedience,
through Jesus Christ our Lord.
Amen.

4. Write the name of each person in the group on a note card. Turn the note cards facedown on the table and let each person take one. This is the person for whom each will pray specifically this week. Before leaving, take a few minutes to visit with the person whose picture you chose, getting to know him/her better. Ask if there are things coming up in that person's life about which you might pray. If participants have cell phones, they may choose to take a picture of the person whose name they chose. Another option involves writing the names of the group members in the front of your workbook. Pray for these persons each week.

Week Two

Pride
"The Spiritual Cancer"

DAY 1

Preoccupation with Self

Vince Lombardi was a famous coach for the Green Bay Packers, a professional football team. He had a monstrous ego, unlimited confidence, and pride that was not always healthy. All sorts of stories exist about him—some true, some apocryphal. One story tells of the occasion when he was in a championship playoff. His wife was not able to go to the game for some reason, and that disappointed Vince. No one thought the Packers were going to win, but against all odds they won the game. You can imagine the coach's exhilaration.

When he came home his wife was already asleep. He tried to slip into bed without awakening her. But when his cold feet touched her legs, she said, "God, your feet are cold." Quick as a flash, the coach replied, "When we are in bed, just call me Vince."

That's a humorous expression of the first of the deadly sins: pride. In *Mere Christianity* C. S. Lewis called pride "the spiritual cancer" which eats up the possibility of love or contentment or even common sense.

From the beginning, when theologians, teachers, and preachers designated the seven deadly sins, every listing puts pride first. In "The Parson's Tale" from *The Canterbury Tales* we are told that the root of all seven deadly sins is "Pride the general root of all harms." The order of their listing may not be as important as the fact expressed by the Parson: They are "all leashed together"; they are "the trunk of the tree from which others branch." I doubt, however, if any of the other seven deadly sins has as great an outflow leading to other expressions of sin as does pride. "The essence of sin is selfishness, and pride is the inordinate assertion of self." (Stalker, p. 4)

The sin of our first parents, Adam and Eve, was pride. Look at Genesis 3:1-5:

Now the serpent was more crafty than any other wild animal that the LORD God had made. He said to the woman, "Did God say, 'You shall not eat from any tree in the garden'?" The woman said to the serpent, "We may eat of the fruit of the trees in the garden; but God said, 'You shall not eat of the fruit of the tree that is in the middle of the garden, nor shall you touch it, or you shall die.'" But the serpent said to the woman, "You will not die; for God knows that when you eat of it your eyes will be opened, and you will be like God, knowing good and evil."

Satan's grabber, "You will be like God," scored its mark. Though there is a rather baffling mystery around the origin of Satan, Revelation 12:7-12 tells about the war that broke out in heaven between Michael and his angels with the "dragon" (serpent) and his angels. Michael and his angels won and "that ancient serpent, who is called the Devil and Satan, the deceiver of the whole world—he was thrown down to the earth" (v. 9).

There is a connection between this New Testament account and the Old Testament prophet Isaiah telling about the fall of the angel Lucifer, the "son of the morning" (Isa. 14:12, KJV).

It was pride that brought the fall. Look at Isaiah 14:13-14:

You said in your heart, "I will ascend to heaven; I will raise my throne above the stars of God; I will sit on the mount of assembly on the heights of Zaphon; I will ascend to the tops of the clouds, I will make myself like the Most High."

There it is—"I will make myself like the Most High"—the same temptation to which Adam and Eve succumbed: "You will be like God" (Gen. 3:5).

So this is the first sin of which we have knowledge. Why did the angels fall? Pride. Milton in *Paradise Lost* pictured the outstanding feature of the leader of the angels in this tragic drama as arrogance. He cries, "Better to reign in hell, than to serve in heav'n."

All of this seems so dramatic, but that's not the way it is with most of us. The way pride usually expresses itself is not dramatic, but it is pervasive. Think of pride as preoccupation with self, the inordinate assertion of self. Stop for a moment and reflect on your life and that of those around you. Do you see why those who have investigated the subject most deeply see pride as the primary sin?

■ ■ ■

Dictionaries give the following as their first definition of pride: "an inordinate self-esteem" (*Webster*); "an unreasonable conceit of superiority . . . an overweening opinion of one's own qualities" (*Oxford English*).

Synonyms for pride are not very attractive: vanity, conceit, arrogance, egotism, self-glorification, boastfulness. Descriptive terms of a more slang nature are bighead, cockiness, stuck-up, snobbishness, self-centered, full of yourself, know-it-all, puffed up. It is no wonder Proverbs says, "Pride goes before destruction, and a haughty spirit before a fall" (Prov. 16:18).

Reflecting and Recording

Reread the synonyms of pride; get them solidly in mind. Now, who is the first person that comes to your mind as a person those words describe? Name that person here. (Remember this is a private journal, and you can be completely honest.)

Now write a paragraph describing this person with special attention to how he/she relates to others.

Spend a little time examining yourself. What characteristics of the person are present in you?

■ ■ ■

Close your time in prayer, asking the Lord to reveal pride in your own life.

During the Day

On page 183, Proverbs 16:18 is printed. Cut it out and put it someplace where you will see it often (your refrigerator door, automobile instrument panel, or your purse or wallet). Read it as often as you see it, memorize it as a reminder of the destructive work of pride in your life.

DAY 2

Superbia: Should We Not Be Proud?

You may be bewildered that pride would be considered one of the seven deadly sins. For some, to think of it as the primary sin, out of which other sins flow, is almost impossible. Should we not be proud?

The Latin word for pride is *superbia* and it means "aiming at what is above." What could be wrong with that? Well, nothing . . . as long as it is that . . . seeking the highest.

Yesterday we gave definitions of pride from two dictionaries. We also listed some synonyms for pride. Turn back and review those.

■ ■ ■

The first definitions of pride in *The American Heritage Dictionary* are quite different: 1) self-respect; 2) elation or satisfaction over one's achievement or possessions.

If pride were only what these definitions describe, it would be something we needed, not something heading the list of seven deadly sins. Think about it. The phrase "She takes no pride in herself" is used to describe someone who is sloppy in her appearance or careless in her work. If the language or action of someone puts another person down, diminishes the person's sense of worth, we say of that person, "He leaves them no pride."

Oppressed and marginalized people are urged to cultivate pride—to be proud of who they are. This is a significant and healthy dimension of the feminist movement. We also remember the refrain that emerged during the 1960s: "Black is beautiful." When we use the word in this fashion, pride is constructive, not destructive. To have a good sense of one's worth is justifiable. Nothing is more needed by most persons than healthy self-esteem and a good measure of self-worth. If we think we are nothing, we will live and act as though we are nothing. We can sin by thinking too slightly or too poorly of ourselves, just as we can by thinking more highly than we ought.

This is a big issue for persons recovering from addictions. Because of their shame and guilt, they have a constant battle with self-pity. Ernie Larsen and Carol Hegarty in *Believing in Myself*, a book of meditations for people in recovery from addiction, said:

> Fostering self-esteem means taking care of ourselves. Often we need to treat ourselves easy, give ourselves the benefit of the doubt, remind ourselves of how far we have come rather than how far we have to go. Yet there is a fine line between sympathizing with our own struggles and wallowing in self-pity.
>
> Self-pity works against self-esteem because it blinds us to reality. Self-pity wears a black veil over its downcast head. Because it never looks up, it sees only part of the picture. And it is only on the anvil of reality that we are able to hammer out something of value. We can't work with what we can't see.
>
> —Larsen and Hegarty, September 3

We doubt if there is a more important factor for recovery from addiction than a solid sense of self-worth. But not only for recovering folks—for all of us. Happiness in life, success in work and relationships are dependent upon our sense of self-worth. That's the reason raising low self-esteem is an essential part of the healing process, not only for those recovering from addictions and dependencies but also for anyone feeling the pain of childhood wounds or other hurts that have crippled us along the way.

So, then, self-worth is a healthy pride—but we must keep our definitions clear. It is OK to be proud of our children, proud of their accomplishment; OK to take pride in our work and to seek to affirm others and cultivate pride in them.

We must be careful, though. Our self-worth is not dependent upon our performance. There is value in what we do, but what we do is not what gives us value. Nor is our worth determined by how we measure up to others. "Good" pride and genuine humility come together when we stop *shaming* and *blaming* ourselves and, at the same time, stop *inflating* ourselves. This can happen when we accept the fact that we are not better or worse than anyone else.

Healthy pride and growth in self-esteem come slowly as we change our perception of ourselves. The power of the Christian faith is precisely at this point: In the sight of God, we are all of eternal value. God created us for Godself, made us a little lower than the angels, and crowned us with glory and honor. (See Psalm 8:3-6.) This is the way Paul put it in his letter to the Romans.

> You did not receive a spirit of slavery to fall back into fear, but you have received a spirit of adoption. When we cry, "Abba! Father!" it is that very Spirit bearing witness with our spirit that we are children of God, and if children, then heirs, heirs of God and joint heirs with Christ.
>
> —Romans 8:15-17

When we accept this description of our identity, the games for position and power which we play are seen for what they are: silly in the least and destructive in the worst.

Reflecting and Recording

Look at the past two months of your life. In three or four sentences describe three occasions, situations, and/or relationships in which you expressed healthy pride.

(1)

(2)

(3)

During the Day

Continue to allow Proverbs 16:18, to which your attention was called yesterday, to "guard" your thinking and action. Seek to identify occasions of healthy and unhealthy pride.

DAY 3

"I" at the Center: The Itch for Recognition

By the grace given to me I say to everyone among you not to think of yourself more highly than you ought to think, but to think with sober judgment, each according to the measure of faith that God has assigned.

—Romans 12:3

Pride is the itch for recognition. It is sin expressed in the need to always put "I" at the center. Chaucer described pride as "a swelling of the heart." How often have we seen it or perhaps experienced it, at least to some degree—a force working in us that makes ourselves the "goal and destination of our own lives' longing." (Holloway, p. 8.)

Take the issue of conversation. "I" at the center expresses itself as a person who cannot speak long without speaking of herself. No matter where the conversation heads, she always brings it back to herself. I experienced this recently when I was telling a person about a violent storm that had come through our town. He couldn't wait for me to finish describing the damage, nor did he ask if anyone had been hurt. When an opening came, he was off and running in his account of a tornado he had braved in Oklahoma.

Persons who are preoccupied with self, who have an itch for recognition, are masters at bringing conversation back to their favorite topic: themselves. It happens in other areas as well.

Have you heard of the meeting of two friends at a party? One of them said, "Have I shown you the pictures of my grandchildren?" The other responded, "No, and I sure appreciate it." When "I" is at the center, what is a part of us or what "belongs" to us takes precedence over everything else. Jokes about pictures of our grandchildren are innocent reminders of where the itch for recognition can take us: to the place where we don't really listen to others; to a preoccupation with self that makes us dull to what's going on around us; to an insensitivity to the needs and concerns of others.

In the extreme, "I" at the center issues in a life of self-pleasing which is inevitably destructive. This is what happened to Narcissus of Greek mythology. He was so vain, so turned in on himself that he spurned the love of the nymph Echo, who grieved herself away to nothing but her voice. To punish Narcissus, the goddess Artemis caused him to stop at a spring to drink. Upon seeing his image in the water Narcissus fell in love with his own reflection; addictively gazing at it, he wasted away from unfufilled love. This is the work of pride. It craves admiration and attention in a fashion that refuses to share the limelight with anyone else.

We will pursue this notion of the exalted love of self more tomorrow. For now, turn briefly to a paradox with which we must grapple.

No scratching of this itch of recognition will soothe it. When we are dealing with self-centeredness, no self-effort can remove the self from the center of its own effort. Trace it in your personal experience. When you seek to control yourself, your attention becomes more fixed on yourself. When you seek to control others in your life, the same thing happens: you remain the center. The harder we work to save ourselves, to correct our faults, the more our attention is centered in self. We can't free ourselves of our own self-centeredness. As we discussed on Day 7 of Week One, Christ alone can do that. Only as we yield ourselves to him, allowing ourselves to be released from our pride, can we be released from our self-centeredness.

Reflecting and Recording

Yesterday you were asked to look at the past two months of your life and describe three occasions, situations, and/or relationships when you expressed "healthy" pride. Look again at the past two months and locate three occasions when "I" at the center was dominant, when an itch for recognition prevailed over concern for others, when self-centeredness brought brokenness and pain.

(1)

(2)

(3)

Do you need to do anything about the experiences you have just described? Tell a person you love her? Ask someone to forgive you? Write a letter? Make a phone call? Offer special prayer? Confess to another? Confess to God? Spend three or four minutes in self-examination.

■ ■ ■

During the Day

Do the things you have just now decided you need to do.

DAY 4

The Tower of Babel and the Towering Self

Now the whole earth had one language and the same words. And as they migrated from the east, they came upon a plain in the land of Shinar and settled there. And they said to one another, "Come, let us make bricks, and burn them thoroughly." And they had brick for stone, and bitumen for mortar. Then they said, "Come, let us build ourselves a city, and a tower with its top in the heavens, and let us make a name for ourselves; otherwise we shall be scattered abroad upon the face of the whole earth."

—Genesis 11:1-4

The proud man sets himself apart by setting himself up. This is what the people sought to do with the Tower of Babel. "Let us make a name for ourselves." That was the sin. There is nothing wrong with building towers and skyscrapers, if the motivation is right.

We are made to live for the glory of God. Our search for significance and meaning, for name and place, must be in the context of our relationship to God.

It is interesting that following this story of the Tower of Babel in Genesis 11, God appealed to Abraham on the basis of making his name great.

Now the LORD said to Abram, "Go from your country and your kindred and your father's house to the land that I will show you. I will make of you a great nation, and I will bless you, and make your name great, so that you will be a blessing. I will bless those who bless you, and the one who curses you I will curse; and in you all the families of the earth shall be blessed."

—Genesis 12:1-3

This was to be achieved, however, in faith and service to God. The failure of the Tower of Babel venture was sinful motivation: "Come, let us make a name for ourselves."

Pride is deadly because it is self-worship. It places one's own interest above the interests of others. So, Lance Webb, in *Conquering the Seven Deadly Sins*, is on target when he says:

> Each of the other six sins in a very definite way is a child of pride. Envy is self-love unable to permit anyone to excel or rise above one's own superiority, with resulting hate, jealousy, intolerance, prejudice, slander, gossip, and use of sarcasm or more violent means of leveling others to one's own height. Anger is self-love striking out with hostility and resentment at those threatening or getting in the way of the fulfillment of the image of one's vision. Dejection is self-love in despair and condemnation of oneself, resulting in apathy, carelessness, unconcern, and boredom. Avarice is self-love seeking to exalt or to forget oneself in material things. Lust and gluttony are self-love seeking to exalt oneself in pleasures and sensual satisfactions, or to escape and forget one's failures and wrongs.
>
> —Webb, pp. 41–42

You get the picture. Pride can be deadly.

Reflecting and Recording

Spend some time thinking about Psalm 51:17: "The sacrifices of God are a broken spirit: a broken and a contrite heart, O God, thou wilt not despise" (KJV). What would it mean for you to have a broken spirit and contrite heart?

■ ■ ■

In what ways do you exhibit pride or self-worship? Spend some time in prayer, confessing your pride, repenting (expressing genuine sorrow, a desire to change), and receiving Christ's forgiveness.

■ ■ ■

During the Day

Check yourself throughout the day with this question: Am I putting my own interests above the needs and interests of others?

DAY 5

Barrier to Salvation

The New Testament tells us that salvation is not something we can earn. We don't merit or deserve, nor can we work for and receive God's love. It is given by God's grace. It comes as a gift. "By grace you have been saved through faith, and this is not your own doing; it is the gift of God" (Eph. 2:8).

It sounds so simple: Salvation is a gift. Yet, strange as it may appear on the surface, the gift can be very threatening, very difficult to receive. Why? Our mind-set is permeated by two thoughts: 1) "You get what you deserve"; and 2) "God helps those who help themselves." Most of us are infected by the fantasy that we are all self-made or that we must work and earn everything that we want or that is essential for life. Are we putting it too strongly? We are infected by pride which says we must "do it ourselves."

So, the most destructive work of pride is that it makes it difficult for us to accept the gift of salvation. It prevents us from receiving the free grace of God. Pride drives us to think we earn our salvation by what we do, that we can be worthy of God's blessing, that we can perform well enough that our heavenly Father will reward us with eternal life.

Jesus' story of the Pharisee and tax collector who go into the Temple to pray is instructive:

Two men went up to the temple to pray, one a Pharisee and the other a tax collector. The Pharisee, standing by himself, was praying thus, "God, I thank you that I am not like other people: thieves, rogues, adulterers, or even like this tax collector. I fast twice a week; I give a tenth of all my income." But the tax collector, standing far off, would not even look up to heaven, but was beating his breast and saying, "God, be merciful to me, a sinner!"

—Luke 18:10-13

The Pharisee can't be saved because he sees no need for salvation. Because pride is the deadly enemy of salvation, it is a sin denounced so often in the Bible. The publican who refuses to raise his head, beats his breast and groans, "God, be merciful to me, a sinner!" is what James Stalker calls "an empty vessel ready to receive the gifts of redeeming love." But what can redeeming love do for the Pharisee who is satisfied with himself and has nothing to pray about but his own merits?

Martin Luther said, "The only thing that resists this idea of justification is the pride of the human heart." Luther's word throbs with personal reality when we remember his story. He was a Roman Catholic monk who spent years trying to gain salvation by exemplary living. Exhausted and disillusioned in his quest, he plummeted into what he called *Anfechtung*. The word is translated "temptation," but we know it as depression. A wise counselor in the monastery prescribed a therapy: He assigned him to teach Paul's letters in the new university at Wittenberg.

With eyes ready to see, a mind ready to understand, and a heart pained—in the anguish of despair, ready to receive any medicine, any resolution to his despair—ready to believe, Luther turned to Romans. He knew what Paul was talking about—it was his own experience he recognized when he read, "I do not do the good I want, but the evil I do not want is what I do" (7:19). And when he read, "All have sinned and fall short of the glory of God; they are now justified by . . . grace as a gift" (3:23-24), he knew God was speaking to him. And the rest is history—his witness and leadership for the Protestant Reformation. So Martin Luther would say it over and over again, in one way or another:

> By the one solid rock we call the doctrine of justification by faith alone, we mean that we are redeemed from sin, death and the devil, and are made partakers of life eternal, not by self-help but by outside help, namely, by the work of the only-begotten Son of God, Jesus Christ alone.
>
> As men without anything—at all, we must wait for the pure mercy of God, we must wait for him to reckon us as righteous and wise.

> —*The Joy of the Saints*, p. 25

Our pride makes it difficult to accept this gift. We want to prove our worth to God by our good deeds and personal achievements. But scripture reminds us that God despises our pride and calls us to trust Jesus Christ, who alone was willing to humble himself as the ultimate servant of humanity, and become obedient "even unto death" (Phil. 2:8, KJV).

Reflecting and Recording

On Day 7 of Week One we discussed the work of grace for salvation in our lives as pardon and power. Spend three or four minutes reflecting on how pride prevents you from receiving God's free pardon.

■ ■ ■

Now spend three or four minutes reflecting on how you try to overcome sin with your own power, rather than yielding yourself or a particular area of your life to Christ to receive his power.

■ ■ ■

During the Day

When you are confronted with temptation today, or when you become aware that you did something wrong, responded in a relationship in an inappropriate way or a way that put another down or brought some sort of pain, call to mind what grace is all about: pardon and power. Receive whichever is appropriate—maybe both.

DAY 6

Pride Worketh Destruction: To Ourselves

A false humility is not a great virtue. It is no more worthy of admiration than a rampant pride. We dealt with this a bit on Day 2, but it needs to be focused on now as we think about the inordinate energy we spend projecting an "image." Depreciating ourselves is as wrong and destructive as esteeming ourselves too much.

In a *Peanuts* cartoon Frieda shouts at Snoopy and essentially tells him that he's not important. Snoopy responds by lying flat on his stomach, his long ears spread out on the ground in dejection. As a dog, he can't speak; but he thinks it and his countenance and body language communicate it: "I'm worthless—I don't even deserve your attention." It's a "dog picture" of the false humility we often project. We confuse the gospel call to self-denial with self-deprecation. Nothing in the gospel calls for a devaluing of self. Someone has said that the "devil's darling sin" is the pride that mimics humility.

Genuine humility is never weak. When we are authentically humble we don't pretend either strength or weakness. We are genuinely strong because we know who we are. We make a big mistake when we begin to think that sinful pride can be overcome through self-contempt. That's not humility. Humility enhances our self-worth and makes us more like Christ, but *humiliation*, self-contempt, diminishes our self-worth and causes us to forget that we are made in the image of God.

Pride is destructive because it *keeps us from knowing the truth about ourselves.* In *Seven Deadly Sins* Tony Campolo tells about a friend who apologizes in such a way as to make himself seem to be innocent.

> On one occasion after deliberately hurting someone with a cutting remark, he apologized by saying, "I'm sorry. I guess I'm too honest for my own good." His pride enabled him to see what he did as a consequence of his virtue rather than an expression of his meanness. On another occasion he marched out of an important conference, leaving the rest of us devastated by his abrupt treatment. Later he apologized by saying, "Please forgive me, but you people were saying intolerable things about me, and I couldn't just sit there and listen to you when I thought you were totally unfair." Once again his nasty behavior was explained away as evidence of his virtue and our shortcomings. He could never recognize any faults in himself.
>
> —Campolo, p. 80

Our pride prevents us from knowing the truth about ourselves. This was the case with a Pharisee about whom Jesus spoke, at which we looked yesterday. Go back and read the story from Luke 18:10-14.

■ ■ ■

The point Jesus made was that there is no help for us unless we are able to acknowledge our own sinfulness. This then is a destructive work of pride against the self: It prevents us from realizing our potential, and it stifles growth because it does not recognize inadequacy. Perhaps the worst expression of pride is spiritual pride. This was the Pharisee's disease. He believed he was already as good and righteous as necessary. Such a disease renders spiritual growth impossible. If you feel no need of further growth, then growth will not come.

Reflecting and Recording

Who is the most humble person you know? Write his or her name here.

Think now—who is the most *falsely* humble person you know? Write his or her name here.

Contrast those two persons, think about their strengths and weaknesses. Is the difference readily obvious?

■ ■ ■

Are there hints of false humility in you? How does this false humility in you express itself?

■ ■ ■

Now spend the balance of your time available in this period examining whether your pride is preventing you from knowing the truth about yourself; and to what degree pride may be stifling your growth because you do not recognize your inadequacy.

■ ■ ■

During the Day

Be vigilant against degrading yourself because you think humility calls for it.

DAY 7

Pride Worketh Destruction in Relationships

If those who are nothing think they are something, they deceive themselves. All must test their own work; then that work, rather than their neighbor's work, will become a cause for pride.

—Galatians 6:3-4

Every time I read that verse I think of a Bantam rooster. I don't know any other creature of God that "thinks it is something, when it is nothing" as does this rooster. It struts around in the barnyard as though it owns the farm. Tiny compared to other chickens and roosters and ducks and turkeys, the Bantam rooster would never admit it. I've seen a Bantam take on the biggest Dominecker rooster in the yard and fight it out. I never read this verse of scripture without thinking of the Bantam, and I never read it without a picture of a seminary professor flashing into my mind. Someone described him as a person who could strut while sitting down. Nothing is more pathetic than that—persons who live lives of pretension, who never look objectively at themselves.

No wonder Paul warned against it. He was echoing the witness of scripture typified in this warning in Proverbs: "When pride comes, then comes disgrace . . . Haughty eyes and a proud heart—the lamp of the wicked—are sin" (Prov. 11:2; 21:4). We see it all the time: pride becoming the seed germ that inflames deeper problems. It causes envy, jealousy, anger, greed, intolerance, and unnecessary worry. Nothing plays havoc in relationships and in Christian community more than an undisciplined pride.

So let's focus on relationships in this last consideration of the deadly sin of pride. Pride is destructive in relationships. As indicated earlier (Day 3), pride is "a swelling of the heart." When the heart swells, filled with its own self-preoccupation and self-pleasure, there is no room for others in it. Having no room for others increases our solitude and we become more and more alone. Convinced of our own abilities and self-sufficiency, we deny that we need community; and even more tragically for others, we refuse to meet the obligations of being in community. Our relationships begin to atrophy.

The destructiveness of pride in relationships is expressed in all sorts of ways. One, it makes us impatient with the faults and failures of others. If we see only the good and perfect in ourselves—which is what pride does—the faults and failures of others are magnified and our impatience prevents understanding and leads to strife in relationship.

As pride makes us see only the good and perfect in ourselves, it also makes us see only the good and perfect in those like us. The result is unhealthy national or ethnic or gender pride, for example. The attributes and characteristics of our own group become magnified so out of proportion that people who are different from us appear in our eyes to be grossly inadequate. Their faults and failures become monumental. Racial strife, gender issues, discrimination, to give just a few examples, vividly illustrate the destructive nature of pride. It begins with individuals and continues its destruction within society.

Two, pride leads to all sorts of presumption. Because we think far more highly of ourselves than we ought to think, we presume on all our relationships. We expect others to cater to our desires. We are unable to see how our selfishness is robbing from another. We are so intent on our own happiness and so centered on getting what we want that we think others should act as we wish. We relate to others and we engage in conversation from a superior stance. Our prideful presumption erects immediate barriers between us and those with whom we desire relationship, as well as even casual acquaintances.

Three, pride prevents our giving attention to others. When I am focused on myself and my own needs being met, it is impossible to give any sustained attention to someone else. Unchecked pride becomes so preoccupied with self that it can neither affirm another nor receive affirmation. The pride-filled person cannot be vulnerable enough to share pain and failure which would elicit the support and affirmation he also needs.

As mentioned earlier, getting pride and humility in balance is essential for addictive folks. There is a connection between unchecked pride and addiction. When persons are lost in their addictive ways, they are driven by self-interest. Neither pride-filled nor addictive persons see outside themselves well enough to ask for help—and so they continue to be trapped in their egos, needing desperately the affirmation they can neither give nor receive.

Four, pride is destructive in our relationship with others and with God because it won't allow us to confess and repent. Pride prevents us from seeing our faults and failures. Yet, when reality breaks through, we are still so controlled by pride that we find it almost impossible to say, "I'm sorry." There is no ongoing relationship with God and with others apart from the healing dynamic of confession and repentance.

Reflecting and Recording

Spend some time taking a personal inventory of the degree to which pride has negatively affected your relationships. Look at each of the results of pride listed here and name persons and situations that have been impacted in different ways. (Remember this is a private journal and you can be honest.)

Impatience

Presumption

Preventing attention and affirmation

Disallowing confession and repentance

Spend some time in prayer, confessing, repenting, and receiving necessary forgiveness for your attitudes and actions recorded here.

■ ■ ■

During the Day

If there is anything you need to do in relation to another person—for example, expressing a specific act of love or asking forgiveness—which has been brought to mind during your reflecting and recording, do so today.

If you are a part of a group using this workbook, this should be your meeting day. Look at the "guide for sharing" on the next pages and make whatever preparation is necessary.

Group Meeting for Week Two

Introduction

Participation in a group such as this is a covenant relationship. You will profit most as you keep the daily discipline of the thirty-minute period and as you faithfully attend these weekly meetings. Do not feel guilty if you have to miss a day in the workbook or be discouraged if you are not able to give the full thirty minutes in daily discipline. Don't hesitate sharing that with the group. We may learn something about ourselves as we share. We may discover, for instance, that we are unconsciously afraid of dealing with the content of a particular day because of what is required and what it reveals about us. Be patient with yourself and always be open to what God may be seeking to teach you.

Our growth, in part, hinges upon our group participation, so share as openly and honestly as you can. Listen to what persons are saying. Sometimes there is meaning beyond the surface of their words which you may pick up if you are attentive.

Being a sensitive participant in this fashion is crucial. Responding immediately to the feelings we pick up is also crucial. Sometimes it is important for the group to focus its entire attention upon a particular individual. If some need or concern is expressed, it may be appropriate for the leader to ask the group to enter into a brief period of special prayer for the persons or concerns revealed. Participants should not always depend upon the leader for this kind of sensitivity;

the leader may miss it. Even if you aren't the leader, don't hesitate to ask the group to join you in special prayer. This praying may be silent, or some person may wish to lead the group in prayer.

Remember, you have a contribution to make to the group. What you consider trivial or unimportant may be just what another person needs to hear. We are not seeking to be profound but simply to share our experience.

Sharing Together

Note: It may not be possible in your time frame to use all the suggestions provided each week. The leader simply selects what will be most beneficial to the group. It is important that the leader be thoroughly familiar with these suggestions in order to move through them selectively according to the direction in which the group is moving and according to the time available. The leader should plan ahead but not hesitate to change the plan according to the nature of the sharing taking place and the needs that emerge.

1. Open your time together with the leader offering a brief prayer of thanksgiving for the opportunity of sharing with the group and petitions for openness in sharing and loving response to each other.
2. Let each person share the most meaningful day in this week's workbook adventure.
3. Now share the most difficult day and tell why it was difficult.
4. Invite two or three persons to share an occasion, interaction, and/or relationship in which they expressed healthy pride (see Day 2).
5. Invite two or three persons to share an occasion when an "itch for recognition" prevailed over concern for others, when self-centeredness brought brokenness and pain.
6. Invite two or three persons to share something they learned about themselves this week.
7. Spend eight to ten minutes discussing these two claims: One, pride is destructive because it keeps us from knowing the truth about ourselves; two, pride stifles growth because it does not recognize inadequacy. Encourage individuals to share personal experiences of this destructive work.
8. Spend three or four minutes discussing this claim: Pride prevents us from giving attention to others. Is there a personal witness in the group of this destructive work of pride?
9. Spend the balance of your sharing time reflecting on and discussing the claim that pride is destructive of our relationship with God and others because it won't allow us to confess and repent.

Praying Together

As stated last week, the effectiveness of this group and the quality of relationship will be enhanced by a commitment to pray for one another by name each day. Place the note cards with names facedown on a table and let each person select a card. This person will be the focus of special prayer for the week. If possible, take pictures of one another for prayer focus in the coming week. Continue this practice throughout your pilgrimage together. Looking at a person's picture or calling the person to mind as you pray for that person will add meaning. Having a picture will remind you that you are to give special prayer attention to this person during the week.

1. Praying corporately each week is a special ministry. Take some time now for a period of verbal prayer. Rehearse some of the sharing that has taken place. If there has been confession, invite a couple of persons to offer a corporate prayer of confession, verbalizing some of those things persons have confessed about pride in their lives and asking the forgiveness of the Lord. Pray that forgiveness will be received.

2. Now allow each person to mention any special needs he or she wishes to share with the entire group. A good pattern is to ask for a period of prayer after each need is mentioned. There may be silent prayer by the entire group, or someone may offer a brief two- or three-sentence verbal prayer.

3. Close your time by praying together the great prayer of the church, the Lord's Prayer. As you pray this prayer, remember that you are linking yourselves with all Christians of all time in universal praise, confession, thanksgiving, and intercession.

Week Three

Envy
"The Sin of the Evil Eye"

As you begin this third week of your journey, here are some thoughts to keep in mind.

Discipline is an important dimension of life. Discipline is not slavish rigidity but an ordering of life that enables you to control your circumstances rather than being controlled by them. For most people, a designated time of meditation and prayer is essential for building a life of prayer.

If you have not yet established a regular time to use this workbook, try to find the right time for you this week. Experiment: in the morning, after work, during the lunch hour, before bedtime. Find time that seems best for you.

If you discover that you can't cover all the workbook material and exercises given for a day, don't berate yourself. Get what you can out of what you do. There is no point in rushing over three or four steps or principles if you cannot think deeply. Consider them seriously one by one, and move only as far as you can.

Intellectual assent to a great principle or possibility is important, but it does us little good until we act upon it—until we say *yes* in our minds, and live it out in relationships.

Don't hesitate to make decisions and resolves, but don't condemn yourself if you fail. God is patient with us and wants us to be patient with ourselves.

DAY 1

Sin Has Its Own Punishment

The word *envy* is from the Latin *invidia*, meaning "to look maliciously upon." The New Testament Greek phrase for envy is literally to have an "evil eye," to look upon with evil. So envy has been called *the sin of the evil eye*. It has within itself its own destructive seed.

There was a man in ancient Greece who killed himself through envy. The story has it that a city erected a statue to honor the champion athlete in its public games. This athlete had an archrival who was so envious that he pledged to destroy the statue. Each night, under the cover of darkness, he would go to the statue and chisel at its base, hoping to make it fall. Finally, he achieved his goal and toppled the statue. His envy had driven him to destruction, not only of the statue but of himself; for when the statue fell, it fell on him.

All sin has its own consequences, its own punishment. Go to Day 5 of Week One and read the portion of the prophet Jeremiah's sermon printed there.

■ ■ ■

The life of the people of Judah was falling apart, their culture crumbling, their family structure collapsing. They were asking why? And Jeremiah answered them without mincing words. Sin. "My people have committed two sins: They have forsaken me, the spring of living water, and have dug their own cisterns, broken cisterns that cannot hold water" (Jer. 2:13, NIV).

At the heart of sin is what Dorothy L. Sayers calls "a deep interior dislocation of human personality." We were created by God, for God. Everything in life should revolve around God. Life will not work wholesomely in any other way. Sin, in all its forms, in one way or another, demands that everything, including God, revolve around "me."

Pride: The itch for recognition—"I" always at the center.
Sloth: Don't bother me. I couldn't care less.
Anger: Don't invade my space. I won't let you get away with that;
            I'll see that you pay.
Avarice: Greed—what's mine is mine.
Lust: My craving must be satisfied.
Gluttony: Give me more and more.
Envy: What's yours should be mine.

Sin, this dislocation of the soul, our refusal to come down off the throne of our life and allow God to have that place, has its own punishment. Jeremiah said, "Your wickedness will punish you" (Jer. 2:19).

The built-in punishment of the sin of envy is that there is no gratification in it; it can enjoy nothing. Envy's appetites never cease. It is insatiable. Coming in through the back door in his definition, Frederick Buechner says in *Wishful Thinking*, "Envy is the consuming desire to have everybody else as unsuccessful as you are."

Envy is the sin of the evil eye. It always sees and desires what it doesn't have. Its punishment is that it will never have what it sees and desires because there will always be more to see than to possess.

Reflecting and Recording

Spend two or three minutes pondering this statement: All sin has its own punishment.

■ ■ ■

Look at your own life. Locate an experience where your sin carried with it its own judgment and punishment. Take enough time to get in touch with the experience and describe it. Record facts—what actually happened—but also feelings.

Spend the balance of your time reflecting on this sentence: Since envy always desires what it doesn't have, it will always go unsatisfied.

■ ■ ■

During the Day

Go through this day with the awareness that envy is the sin of the evil eye. Pay attention to how you look at things, what you desire, and why you desire it.

DAY 2

The Sin No One Confesses

Envy has been called the nastiest, ugliest, meanest, and most grim of the seven deadly sins. Have you ever known a person to confess envy? We talk about our pride, our laziness, our anger, even our lust, greed, and gluttony, but who is willing to admit that they are envious? We put forth effort to give some of the deadly sins—pride, anger, sloth—a positive twist, but there is no way to do that with envy. We joke about the other deadly sins, but we have never heard a joke about envy. It is a grim reality with no redeeming virtue.

The other sins are primarily against a particular virtue—pride is against humility, gluttony is against temperance—but, as Chaucer's Parson reminds us, envy is "a foul sin, . . . the worst that is," because it sneers "against all virtues and against all goodnesses." The writer of Proverbs gives envy this perspective: "A sound heart is life to the body, but envy is rottenness to the bones" (Prov. 14:30, NKJV). "Wrath is cruel and anger a torrent, but who is able to stand before jealousy?" (Prov. 27:4, NKJV).

Paul names envy as one of the works of the flesh which can have no place in the kingdom of God.

Live by the Spirit, I say, and do not gratify the desires of the flesh. For what the flesh desires is opposed to the Spirit, and what the Spirit desires is opposed to the flesh; for these are opposed to each other, to prevent you from doing what you want. But if you are led by the Spirit, you are not subject to the law. Now the works of the flesh are obvious: fornication, impurity, licentiousness, idolatry, sorcery, enmities, strife, jealousy, anger, quarrels, dissensions, factions, envy, drunkenness, carousing, and things like these. I am warning you, as I warned you before: those who do such things will not inherit the kingdom of God.

—Galatians 5:16-21

While envy is the sin no one confesses, it is the sin of which most of us are guilty. Let's test it at an elementary level—making comparisons. Comparing ourselves to others and desiring what they have or wanting to be who they are is the heart of envy. Do you find yourself thinking this?

- "I wish I were as smart as she."
- "Oh, to be handsome like he is!"
- "Why can't I be as athletic as she?"
- "If only I had his connections."

We could add to the list. These verbalizations are common, and seem so innocent. But you have only to scratch a bit beneath the surface to identify a symptom of a larger problem. These questions will help: What is the purpose of comparison? What are we really doing when we compare ourselves with others? If we are gathering interesting information, that's one thing. But if the real issue is comparing ourselves to others because we question our own adequacy, then we have located a real problem. If we are always making comparisons, we are going to come out on the short end of the stick.

Reflecting and Recording

In the other days of this week we will deal with different facets of envy and its destructive payoff in our life. For now let's reflect on two areas. Spend some time thinking about the following two questions.

(1) Do you ever look at another person and wish you could be like her or him? Stay with the question with probing honesty for two or three minutes.

(2) Probe a bit deeper. If envy is "the sorrow at another's success and the joy over another's misfortune," have you ever been guilty of envy? Again spend some time probing and assessing past and present attitudes and experiences.

An antidote for the jealousy that drives us to compare ourselves to others is to become convinced that we are persons of worth and that our value does not depend upon how we compare to others. How convinced are you of that?

■ ■ ■

Close your time with prayer, offering yourself to God as you are and accepting the grace of God's acceptance of you as you are.

During the Day

On page 183 this affirmation is printed: I Am a Unique, Unrepeatable Miracle of God. Cut it out and place it somewhere (bathroom mirror, refrigerator door, instrument panel of your car) where you can see it often. Claim the truth of it. Repeat it to yourself in the next few days until you memorize it. Pray that the Lord will enable you to be convinced of the truth of your worth.

DAY 3

Color Me Green

Red with anger. Purple with rage. Green with envy. Green may be your favorite color, but you don't want to turn green. We associate sickness with our complexion turning green.

"The grass is always greener on the other side of the fence." We never connected this common platitude with envy until we began research for this workbook. The connection lies there in plain sight—what is out there or over there or beyond what we have is what we want. We envy it.

As we suggested yesterday, envy is the sin no one confesses but of which most of us are guilty. We may be free of lust, free of sloth, free of gluttony, perhaps free of pride and greed, but who is free of envy? We may not be totally green with envy, but who does not at least contain an olive spot here or there?

There are some common symptoms of envy which will help us identify its presence. Malice is one. "Ill will with a desire to harm" is the way the dictionary defines this symptom of envy. It's one of the most conspicuous expressions of envy. "They sought to ruin his reputation by pure malice" is a sentence that captures the meaning. Envy chips away at the reputation of another by innuendo and half-truth—in one breath praising, in another damning—always underscoring the defects of another though veiling it with a compliment: "He is a marvelous speaker, charming, loves the limelight, would be wonderful to have a conversation with if he didn't talk all the time."

Another symptom of envy is jealousy. Most commonly, envy is a sin among equals. Preachers are most apt to be envious and thus jealous of other preachers. Doctors are more likely to be jealous of a surgeon than of a poet. An auto mechanic isn't usually jealous of a carpenter. A clear example of jealousy in the Bible is in the Old Testament story of King Saul. Here is a part of the story:

> David went out and was successful wherever Saul sent him; as a result, Saul set him over the army. And all the people, even the servants of Saul, approved. As they were coming home, when David returned from killing the Philistine, the women came out of all the towns of Israel, singing and dancing, to meet King Saul, with tambourines, with songs of joy, and with musical instruments. And the women sang to one another as they made merry, "Saul has killed his thousands, and David his ten thousands." Saul was very angry, for this saying displeased him. He said, "They have ascribed to David ten thousands, and to me they have ascribed thousands; what more can he have but the kingdom?" So Saul eyed David from that day on.
>
> —1 Samuel 18:5-9

Isn't that a telling sentence? "Saul eyed David from that day on." He was jealous not of the many gifts of David but because of David's accomplishments as a warrior. This is where he threatened Saul. Saul's jealousy grew; his eye became so evil that he sought to kill David.

A third symptom of envy is dejection. Basically, envy is sorrow for another's good; but it can also cause us to be sorrowful over our own lack of good:

- the blessing and popularity of a friend may cause us to be depressed;
- the good looks of a sister or a brother may bring dejection in us;
- the brilliance and success of a colleague may cause us to question ourselves and produce a sense of failure—thus dejection.

A fourth symptom of envy is hypocrisy. The apostle Paul admonishes us to "rejoice with those who rejoice, weep with those who weep" (Rom. 12:15). Envy causes us to do a flip-flop: we rejoice when others weep, and we weep when others rejoice. Less extreme, envy prevents us from rejoicing sincerely. So we become hypocritical. We pretend happiness and joy when good things happen to others and don't happen to us, but it is only pretension.

Thus a final symptom—perhaps an accumulation of all the rest—is lovelessness. Though envy begins in self-love, wanting something for self, the envious person ends up not loving herself. This lack of loving oneself goes beyond dejection to self-contempt. When we are burdened with self-contempt, we have neither desire nor energy to love another person.

Reflecting and Recording

Thomas Fuller wrote the following prayer in the seventeenth century:

Lord, I perceive my soul deeply guilty of envy.
I had rather thy work were undone than done better by another than by myself.
Dispossess me, Lord, of this spirit
And turn my envy into holy emulation;
Yes, make other men's gifts to be mine, by making me thankful to thee for them.

—Holloway, p. 21

Read the prayer thoughtfully again.

■ ■ ■

Write a prayer of confession, owning the way you have been "green with envy," giving expression to any symptoms of envy in your life, and asking God for deliverance.

During the Day

Again go through the day, paying attention to how you look at things, what and why you desire something.

DAY 4

A Black Spot in Our Sunshine

I sat at dinner recently with three dear people in my life. They knew I was preoccupied with this work on the seven deadly sins, so they questioned me. "Which sin are you working on?"

I took advantage of the opening. "Envy," I said, "and would you mind talking about it?"

"Not at all," said one, "since we are not talking about gluttony."

"Would each of you share some occasion of envy in your life—either one-time, or ongoing?"

"First, define it," came a quick response.

"We'll keep it elementary—basic," I said. "You see something that someone else has, which you desperately want; you feel bad that he has it and you don't. You sometimes even find yourself having bad feelings toward the other person—but basically, it's just a matter of wanting something someone else has and you don't."

It took a bit of sifting, but not a whole lot of conversation, for each of us to locate a major point of envy. One person was overweight and constantly fighting that battle. She admitted being envious of another person in the group who could eat whatever she pleased, and as much as she wanted, without ever gaining weight.

Another's face clouded as he said, "I'm envious of my brother. He is happy-go-lucky, always the charming person in a group, can laugh and make others laugh. I often resent that I'm a type A personality, intense, serious. I find it hard to let my hair down and relax. I wish I were more like him."

It took a bit more probing for the third person. She mentioned some things, and then her husband asked, "What about our conversation earlier today?" That triggered it. She admitted her envy of mothers who have a close, intimate, joyful relationship with their daughters. She and her daughter love each other. There is no estrangement, but they are so different they find it difficult to sustain communication and discover points of linkage and bonding.

If you knew these three persons as I do, you would probably envy something in them. All of them are committed Christians. The man has been a great success in business and is wealthy. The women are charming, attractive, fun to be with, and gifted in obvious ways. Yet, they have what Thomas Carlyle called "a black spot in our sunshine." (Holloway, pp. 17–18)

Envy is present in all of us. No matter who we are or what we have accomplished or the goods we have accumulated, the bright sunshine of life is often blotted by a dark spot of envy.

Viewing sin from biblical chronology, envy is the second of the deadly sins. Pride was the first, leading to Adam and Eve's expulsion from the garden. Envy came next, resulting in Cain's murder of his brother Abel. The next dramatic biblical occasion of envy occurred with the brothers of Joseph. They were jealous of Joseph's relationship with their father; they envied his coat of many colors. Here is a part of that story:

So Joseph went after his brothers, and found them at Dothan. They saw him from a distance, and before he came near to them, they conspired to kill him. They said to one another, "Here comes this dreamer. Come now, let us kill him and throw him into one of the pits; then we shall say that a wild animal has devoured him, and we shall see what will become of his dreams." But when Reuben heard it, he delivered him out of their hands, saying, "Let us not take his life." Reuben said to them, "Shed no blood; throw him into this pit here in the wilderness, but lay no hand on him"—that he might rescue him out of their hand and restore him to his father. So when Joseph came to his brothers, they stripped him of his robe, the long robe with sleeves that he wore; and they took him and threw him into a pit.

—Genesis 37:17-24

Scripture doesn't give all the information, but we can fill in the blanks. It wasn't that the father didn't love all the sons. It wasn't that he did not provide equally for them, or that they were insecure in the family. They did not go lacking, nor was the father abusive.

Yes, there was obvious favoritism—but not enough to bring abuse and suffering to the rest. The coat of many colors and the father's special love were too much for them to take. Their jealousy issued in anger and explosive passion. They would have killed Joseph had a caravan not intervened, giving them the opportunity to see a more "profitable" way to rid themselves of Joseph by selling him into slavery.

The "black spot in our sunshine," our envy, may not blossom into violence, or destructive action against another—though sometimes it does. However, it always does violence to us. It robs us of joy. It becomes a barrier to the celebration of who we are. It blinds us to our blessings. We lose perspective, focusing on what we don't have, thus we don't affirm and cultivate the gifts that are ours.

Reflecting and Recording

If you had been at dinner with me, along with the three persons about whom I wrote, what would be your confession of envy? Record that confession here.

How has this particular envy negatively impacted your life? Make enough notes to bring the issue into clear perspective.

During the Day

Continue claiming the affirmation: *I am a unique, unrepeatable miracle of God.*

DAY 5

The Gallows of Envy

The movie *Amadeus* presented a vivid picture of the life and times of Wolfgang Amadeus Mozart. In the movie we meet Antonio Salieri, the court musician to the Emperor Joseph of Austria in Vienna. He had dedicated himself to serving God and had as his only goal to bring glory to God through his music. All of his life, he dreamed that his music would inspire people toward heaven. He prayed that God would enable him to compose music that would reflect God's glory. Unfortunately, Salieri had not been blessed with those gifts. His music was pleasant and enjoyable; his listeners were always entertained, but his compositions were not masterpieces. Then Salieri met Mozart and his own mediocrity became glaringly apparent.

Young Mozart was crude, childish, obscene, and lewd. Yet, he was obviously also blessed with extraordinary talent. He was a virtuoso on the harpsichord, dazzling all who heard him play. His music was intricate, moving, thrilling; it illustrated at every turn Mozart's mastery of virtually all forms of composition. Even though Salieri was very popular, he recognized that his talent was ordinary and that most of his work would not be remembered. As Mozart's fame grew, so did Salieri's envy. He coveted Mozart's gifts, became obsessed with him, and began to plot ways to destroy him. Salieri was successful inasmuch as Mozart did die very young; yet he paid a hefty price for that success. Salieri's obsessive envy eventually drove him insane.

The final climactic scene is tragic. Salieri, only a shell of his former self, is left living amidst the grime and filth of an insane asylum. In a last moving monologue, Salieri curses God for denying him the kind of talent that he granted to Mozart.

Envy was deadly to Salieri. It alienated him from God and drove him insane. Extreme? Yes, but a sober lesson of the seriousness of this sin of the evil eye.

There is a Bible narrative with an ironic twist that likewise paints a picture of envy's deadly work in our life. Haman was the most powerful confidant and servant of King Ahasuerus of Persia. Mordecai was a porter at the king's gate, not a place of honor at all, and in no way comparable to the position held by Haman. Haman saw in Mordecai courage and integrity that he didn't have. While all the servants lay flat on their faces as the king passed by, Mordecai stood erect; nor would he bow to Haman.

Mordecai's dignity, even in his low state, enraged Haman. His envy of Mordecai became a burning passion to the point that he devised a plot to destroy the Jews, of which Mordecai was the champion. Haman built a gallows on which to hang Mordecai. Here comes the twist of irony. Mordecai discovered Haman's plot to destroy the Jews and made the case to Queen Esther, herself a Jew, that she must save her people. His famous words to the Queen have echoed down through history to challenge all who may be in a potential place of influence: "Perhaps you have come . . . for just such a time as this" (Esth. 4:14). Esther risked her life to save her people.

So the king and Haman went in to feast with Queen Esther. On the second day, as they were drinking wine, the king again said to Esther, "What is your petition, Queen Esther? It shall be granted you. And what is your request? Even to the half of my kingdom, it shall be fulfilled." Then Queen Esther answered, "If I have won your favor, O king, and if it pleases the king, let my life be given me—that is my petition—and the lives of my people—that is my request. For we have been sold, I and my people, to be destroyed, to be killed, and to be annihilated. If we had been sold merely as slaves, men and women, I would have held my peace; but no enemy can compensate for this damage to the king." Then King Ahasuerus said to Queen Esther, "Who is he, and where is he, who has presumed to do this?" Esther said, "A foe and enemy, this wicked Haman!" Then Haman was terrified before the king and the queen. The king rose from the feast in wrath and went into the palace garden, but Haman stayed to beg his life from Queen Esther, for he saw that the king had determined to destroy him. When the king returned from the palace garden to the banquet hall, Haman had thrown himself on the couch where Esther was reclining; and the king said, "Will he even assault the queen in my presence, in my own house?" As the words left the mouth of the king, they covered Haman's face. Then Harbona, one of the eunuchs in attendance on the king, said, "Look, the very gallows that Haman has prepared for Mordecai, whose word saved the king, stands at Haman's house, fifty cubits high." And the king said, "Hang him on that." So they hanged Haman on the gallows that he had prepared for Mordecai. Then the anger of the king abated.

—Esther 7

Extreme? Yes. Haman died on the gallows of envy that he had prepared for another. Our envy can be the gallows on which we hang because envy is destructive.

Envy is a major cause of unhappiness. Those who envy are never happy with what they have. Envy brings self-contempt. We despise ourselves because we are not the persons we envy. We loathe ourselves for not possessing what those we envy possess.

Extreme envy does not simply desire the kinds of things another has. The envious person wants to take what he desires from the other, and if he can't have it solely for himself, he may do everything possible to strip the other of it.

On Day 3 we discussed a form of malice that seeks to destroy another person's reputation. Gossip and backbiting are thus chief expressions of envy. The artist Giotto di Bondone painted envy as a man with large ears, listening for any hint of rumor or scandal, and a serpent tongue to poison and deface another person's reputation. Tarnishing another's good name is a way of destroying him and is tantamount to murder as an offense against him.

Envy is deadly, not just because it sometimes literally destroys us but because it will not let us live. It will not let us be satisfied with what we have or be grateful for our talents and personal qualities. Envy hinders us from finding meaning in who we are and making the best and rewarding use of our gifts.

Reflecting and Recording

Think of family members and acquaintances you know well. Is there one who has allowed his or her envy to hurt and harm another? Name and describe that person's envy and its result.

Is there one who has allowed envy to be harmful, perhaps destructive to himself? Name and describe that person's envy and its result.

Pray for the persons you have named and pray that God will continue to reveal when you are most vulnerable to envy.

■ ■ ■

During the Day

As you claim that you are a unique, unrepeatable miracle of God, pray that the persons you named above will also own that truth for themselves.

DAY 6

Roots of Envy and Covetousness

There is no distinction, since all have sinned and fall short of the glory of God; they are now justified by his grace as a gift, through the redemption that is in Christ Jesus, whom God put forward as a sacrifice of atonement by his blood, effective through faith. He did this to show his righteousness, because in his divine forbearance he had passed over the sins previously committed; it was to prove at the present time that he himself is righteous and that he justifies the one who has faith in Jesus.

—Romans 3:22-26

On Day 4 I shared a dinner conversation where three dear people in my life talked about envy. I could not have asked them to confess their envy without being willing, in fact, "going first," to confess mine.

For a good part of my life I have been envious of persons who have an "excellent education." I'm speaking of formal education. I grew up in poverty. My parents didn't go to high school; none of my siblings or cousins went to college. I finished college and graduated from theology school, but my focus was not on education. I was intent primarily on getting the degrees required for my ordination as a minister in The Methodist Church, graduating and getting on with the preaching ministry to which God had called me.

In high school, college, and graduate school I envied those who had what I deemed great cultural and educational opportunities. I felt cheated—economically, culturally, and educationally deprived. My envy flowed out of a deep, seething anger at the way life had cheated me.

I chose to work part-time as a pastor while in college and seminary, giving more time to serving the congregations than to my studies, which should have been primary. I was not long out of graduate school, serving full-time in the church, before I knew I had made a mistake. I have had to play catch-up ever since. Thus has been my ongoing envy of those who had an "excellent education."

It took a long time for me personally to own, to admit to myself, and to confess to the Lord what should have been obvious. At the root of envy and covetousness is a terrible sense of inadequacy and inferiority.

Somewhere along the way, I made a shocking discovery. It came through my pastoral counseling. It dawned on me that a compulsive womanizer with whom I was counseling was suffering from the same terrible sense of inadequacy and inferiority as I. As often as not, he was more guilty of covetousness than of lust because of his need to cover up his anxiety and fear. Power over women was his sick game of pretension and machoism.

It is a jolting thing when the truth finally grips your awareness. It was one thing to preach from my lofty pulpit that "all have sinned and fall short of the glory of God" (Rom. 3:23). It was quite another to own and confess—to live with the reality and deal with the fact—that what makes you envious of the person with an excellent education is the same thing that makes a man seek a "new" woman to conquer.

Our envy or covetousness is never satisfied. Advertisers know this. Millions of dollars are spent daily in the United States, holding out the promise of happiness, satisfaction, and meaning, appealing mostly to the residual presence of the seven deadly sins in our life—certainly appealing to our need to feel adequate, sufficient, powerful, accepted, and appreciated.

The only satisfaction for what leads to envy and covetousness is the redeeming knowledge that we are loved and accepted by God as we are, with all our weaknesses and inadequacies. As good parents do not require their children to be brilliant, talented, accomplished, and successful before accepting them, so our heavenly Father accepts us. Even when we are unacceptable in our own eyes, God accepts us.

Paul's word to the Romans is a clear statement that it is not our goodness or righteousness that saves—only our faith in what God has done for us in Jesus Christ. It also states clearly that we are "all in the same boat"—all sinners, constantly falling short of the glory of God. Paul makes the case a bit differently.

> While we were still weak, at the right time Christ died for the ungodly. Indeed, rarely will anyone die for a righteous person—though perhaps for a good person someone might actually dare to die. But God proves his love for us in that while we still were sinners Christ died for us. Much more surely then, now that we have been justified by his blood, will we be saved through him from the wrath of God. For if while we were enemies, we were reconciled to God through the death of his Son, much more surely, having been reconciled, will we be saved by his life.
>
> —Romans 5:6-10

That should convince us. Even when we are unacceptable in our own eyes, God accepts us. We do not have to be brilliant, or successful, or good. We have only to claim our position as God's children. Relaxing in the confidence of God's love and acceptance, we learn to affirm and accept ourselves; thus the root causes of envy and covetousness are nullified.

Reflecting and Recording

Go back to Day 4 and remind yourself of the envy you confessed in your reflecting and recording.

■ ■ ■

Now go back to your reflecting and recording yesterday and remind yourself of the two persons whose envy you described.

■ ■ ■

Did your envy or that of the two persons you named flow out of a terrible sense of inadequacy or inferiority? Did the envy have any connection with a deep longing to be recognized, accepted, appreciated, and valued?

■ ■ ■

Pray this prayer in closing:

> Grant, O Lord, that as I remember the kindness which I have received and never merited, and the punishments which I have deserved and never suffered, I may give thanks to you for your unfailing mercies and for the mercies of my sisters and brothers through Jesus Christ our Lord. Amen.

During the Day

Call at least one person today and tell her that she is a unique, unrepeatable miracle of God. If she asks what motivated you to make the call, tell her.

DAY 7

The Denial of the Goodness and Mercy of God

The kingdom of heaven is like a landowner who went out early in the morning to hire laborers for his vineyard. After agreeing with the laborers for the usual daily wage, he sent them into his vineyard. When he went out about nine o'clock, he saw others standing idle in the marketplace; and he said to them, "You also go into the vineyard, and I will pay you whatever is right.' So they went. When he went out again about noon and about three o'clock, he did the same. And about five o'clock he went out and found others standing around; and he said to them, "Why are you standing here idle all day?" They said to him, "Because no one has hired us." He said to them, "You also go into the vineyard." When evening came, the owner of the vineyard said to his manager, "Call the laborers and give them their pay, beginning with the last and then going to the first." When those hired about five o'clock came, each of them received the usual daily wage. Now when the first came, they thought they would receive more; but each of them also received the usual daily wage. And when they received it, they grumbled against the landowner, saying, "These last worked only one hour, and you have made them equal to us who have borne the burden of the day and the scorching heat." But he replied to one of them, "Friend, I am doing you no wrong; did you not agree with me for the usual daily wage? Take what belongs to you and go; I choose to give to this last the same as I give to you. Am I not allowed to do what I choose with what belongs to me? Or are you envious because I am generous?" So the last will be first, and the first will be last.

—Matthew 20:1-16

It is an unsettling story. It certainly doesn't make economic sense and it violates a common sense of fairness. We can't be too harsh on the workers who grumbled and murmured about what seemed injustice to them.

Jesus did not stutter, nor was he hesitant in confronting the grumblers with their sin. His question was a probing one: "Are you envious because I am generous?"

Envy is calculating; love and mercy are not. No injustice had been done. Everyone had been paid what they had been promised. Some of the workers were not satisfied with their just pay; they were jealous of those who had received more than they had justly earned.

Envy refuses to recognize God's goodness to us. The landowner had been good to the workers, had paid them well for their labor. Yet, when they saw the good fortune of those who received as much for working less, their jealousy blinded them to what was theirs and how good it was when not diminished by comparing it to others. Not only does envy refuse to recognize God's goodness to us, it refuses to rejoice in God's goodness to others.

Think about it. Is not what you envy in another person God's gifts to him or her? Personality, talent, intelligence, good looks, charm, grace, wit, creativity. And you can count on it: What others find enviable about you is also God's gifting.

The medieval word for generous gifts is *largesse*. Envy denies God's extravagant *largesse*.

Envy is so malicious that it does not restrict itself to desiring what others have, to being sorrowful over another's success and joyful over their failure, to using unworthy means to acquire what it covets; it often takes a strange twist in our lives: We desire others to envy us. Tony Campolo reminds us of a sick kind of psychological fulfillment that comes from being envied.

> Thorstein Veblen, one of America's most brilliant economic theorists, claims that the spending habits of people are highly influenced by the psychic enjoyment which comes from getting others to long for what they possess. It is Veblen's contention that it is possible to get people to buy products that are not particularly superior in quality, by publicizing widely that the products are very expensive. This practice, which Veblen calls conspicuous consumption, motivates people to buy expensive automobiles because the buyers know that most other people in the society know that these cars are very expensive.
>
> —Campolo, pp. 96–97

The antidote to envy begins with kindling our love of God and affirming God's mercy and goodness. Acknowledging and committing ourselves to God's love, we can root out envy by first accepting ourselves and God's gifts, however modest or abundant, making the most of them, and cultivating a sense of gratitude and generosity.

Karl A. Olsson puts it in this perspective: Envy melts before the truth of God's generosity.

> Hence sanctification begins in praising God for the gifts he has given men. I do not resent the gift; I adore the Giver. God be thanked for the intelligence of Colleague Abel! God be thanked for the success of Competitor Baker! May the Lord be praised for making Brother Charlie so effective in the pulpit! Praise the Lord for the unspoiled loveliness of Sister Dolly! How good of God to shower such talent on Neighbor Easy's children!
>
> —Olsson, p. 26

Another way of rooting out envy is to utilize our God-given wisdom and ability to reason. When we look closely at the circumstances of the persons and things we envy, we will often discover they may not actually merit that response after all. A story from the Taoist literature of ancient China illustrates this well:

> There once was a wise man who owned several beautiful horses. One horse, in particular, was so fast and strong and magnificent that it evoked the envy of the man's neighbor. Unfortunately, one day the horse broke free and ran into the hills. At once the neighbor's attitude changed from envy to pity at the man's loss, but the wise man said, "Who knows if I should be pitied or if I should be envied because of this?"
>
> The next day, the horse returned to the wise man leading a herd of fifty equally magnificent wild horses with him. The neighbor was again filled with envy, but again

the wise man said, "Who knows if I should be envied or if I should be pitied because of this?" Not long after he had said this, his only son tried to ride one of the wild horses but was thrown off and broke his leg. Again, the neighbor's envy changed to pity, but the wise man answered once more, "Who knows if I should be pitied or if I should be envied because of this?"

The following day, an officer in the emperor's army came to draft the man's son for an extremely hazardous mission. Because his leg was broken, he was relieved of the responsibility for the assignment that would almost certainly have meant death. The neighbor's son was taken in his place and as a result, he once again envied the wise man. As he had before, the wise man responded, "Who knows if I should be envied or if I should be pitied because of this?"

The story continues in this same way with the neighbor's emotions shifting from envy to pity and back again as the events unfold. It doesn't take long to see the point of the story: Things are not always what they seem. What on the surface appears to be very desirable may actually be something that brings us great suffering and anguish. Conversely, circumstances that initially seem to be difficult or unfavorable may prove to be very rewarding. God has blessed us with common sense and wisdom. If we use those gifts, we will be able to combat our inclinations toward envy more effectively.

The surest way of rooting out envy is to rely on the strength only Christ can provide. We can strive to acknowledge God's love and accept ourselves and God's gifts. We can strive to cultivate a sense of gratitude and generosity and utilize our ability to reason. But only through the strength Christ provides will our striving be successful. Because envy is the deadly sin most common to all, we certainly need help beyond ourselves in dealing with it. We need the mercy and grace of Christ: mercy as forgiveness and grace as power. We must claim the assurance of Paul: "I can do all things through [Christ] who strengthens me" (Phil. 4:13).

Reflecting and Recording

Spend some time reflecting on this entire week's consideration of envy. You may want to simply scan the pages, noting what you may have underlined, or what you have written in your reflecting and recording.

■ ■ ■

As a result of insight you may have received or awareness of envy's presence in your life, is there some person that you need to talk with? Perhaps you have hurt someone by your envy. Do you need to ask forgiveness? Do you need to find some person you trust with whom you are willing to share occasions of envy? Remember, a part of our dealing with envy is acknowledging and naming it.

■ ■ ■

During the Day

Act on what you have just concluded in your time of reflection.

Group Meeting for Week Three

Introduction

Two essential ingredients for a Christian fellowship are feedback and follow-up. Feedback is necessary to keep the group dynamic working positively for all participants. Follow-up is essential to express Christian concern and ministry.

The leader is primarily responsible for feedback in the group. All persons should be encouraged to share their feelings about how the group is functioning. Listening is crucial. To listen to another, as much as any other action, is a means of affirming that person. When we listen to another, we are saying, "You are important; I value you." It is also crucial to check out meaning in order that those who are sharing this pilgrimage may know that we really hear. We often mishear. "Are you saying——?" is a good check question. It takes only a couple of persons in a group who listen and give feedback in this fashion to set the mood for the group.

Follow-up is the function of everyone. If we listen to what others are saying, we will discover needs and concerns beneath the surface, situations that deserve special prayer and attention. Make notes of these as the group shares. Follow up during the week with a telephone call, a written note of caring and encouragement, a visit. What distinguishes Christian fellowship is caring in action. "My, how those Christians love one another!" So follow up each week with others in the group.

Sharing Together

By this time, a significant amount of "knowing" exists in the group. Persons are feeling safe in the group, perhaps more willing to share. Still, there is no place for pressure. The leader, however, should be especially sensitive to those slow to share. Seek gently to coax them out. Every person is a gift to the group. The gift is fully revealed by sharing.

1. Begin your meeting with a time of prayer. Ask two or three persons to share the prayers they wrote on Day 3 of this week. It will be helpful if the leader asks some persons ahead of time to do this.
2. Spend ten to fifteen minutes talking about the symptoms of envy. Take the symptoms each in turn. Begin the discussion by reading what is said about each in Day Three: malice, jealousy, dejection, hypocrisy, and lovelessness.
3. On Day 4 I shared the confessions of three people and on Day 6 my own confession about envy. Invite three or four persons to share how envy has expressed itself in them.

4. Spend a few minutes discussing the claim that all sin has its own punishment. Relate the discussion especially to pride and envy.
5. The most elementary level of envy is making comparisons—comparing ourselves to others and desiring what they have, or wanting to be who they are. Invite all who will to share in a few sentences how this has been present in their life.
6. The story of Antonio Salieri in *Amadeus* is a dramatic example of the destructive power of envy. Who can recall stories where envy has been destructive? Maybe two or three experiences can be shared. (Refer to your Reflecting and Recording on Day 5.)
7. Spend a few minutes talking about the strange twist envy sometimes takes: We desire others to envy us. To begin the discussion, invite someone to read aloud for the group the reference from Tony Campolo (p. 71).
8. Along with acknowledging God's love and acceptance of us as we are, the following is ammunition to combat envy: pay attention to and stay aware of God's generosity; call on wisdom for discernment—things are not always what they seem; rely on the strength only Christ can provide. Spend the balance of your sharing time talking about how you can use this ammunition to combat envy.

Praying Together

1. The leader should take up the instant photos of the group, shuffle them, and let each person draw a new one.
2. Invite each member of the group to spend two minutes in quiet prayer for the person whose picture he or she has drawn, focusing on what the person has shared in this meeting.
3. Invite the group to turn to page 62 of the workbook, to the prayer of Thomas Fuller. Let the group pray the prayer in unison.
4. Close the time with sentence prayers, praying specifically about the needs shared by persons when they talked about their struggles with envy, as well as other needs that have been expressed. The leader will offer final prayer.

Week Four

Anger
"The Devil's Furnace"

DAY 1

Two Pictures of Anger

The short story "The Convert," by historian, critic, poet, and essayist Lerone Bennett, Jr., is his story of two African American men in Mississippi. In a sense it is the story of every person. It is also the story of sin and redemption.

In the story, published in *Mississippi Writers: Reflections of Childhood and Youth* edited by Dorothy Abbott, Aaron Lott is the pastor of Rock of Zion Baptist Church. Booker Brown is a deacon in the church and the owner of the funeral home. Bennett tells the story from Brother Booker's viewpoint. When Aaron announces that he is going to the Baptist Convention and he isn't going to travel Jim Crow, Brother Booker tries to talk him out of it. Booker walks with him to the train station, reasoning, cajoling, pleading, but to no avail.

There is an awful scene at the train station, and Booker witnesses it all from the "colored waiting room." When Sheriff Sampson comes the die is cast:

"I'm gonna give you a chance, preacher. Git on over to the n———r side and git quick."
"I ain't bothering nobody, Mr. Sampson."
Somebody in the crowd yelled: "Don't reason wit' the n———r, Bull. Hit 'im."
Mr. Sampson walked up to Aaron and grabbed him in the collar and threw him up against the ticket counter. He pulled out his gun.
"Did you hear me, deacon. I said, 'Git.'"
"I'm going to St. Louis, Mr. Sampson. That's cross state lines.
The court done said ————"

Aaron didn't have a chance. The blow came from nowhere. Laying there on the floor with blood spurting from his mouth, Aaron looked up at Mr. Sampson and he did another crazy thing: He grinned. Bull Sampson jumped up in the air and came down on Aaron with all his two hundred pounds. It made a crunchy sound. He jumped again and the mob, maddened by the blood and heat, moved in to help him. They fell on Aaron like mad dogs. They beat him with chairs; they beat him with sticks; they beat him with guns.

—Abbott, p. 48

77

A story in the book of Acts recounts the same kind of anger and rage. Stephen had done great wonders and signs among his people, so the religious leaders plotted against him.

> Then they secretly instigated some men to say, "We have heard him speak blasphemous words against Moses and God." They stirred up the people as well as the elders and the scribes; then they suddenly confronted him, seized him, and brought him before the council. They set up false witnesses who said, "This man never stops saying things against this holy place and the law; for we have heard him say that this Jesus of Nazareth will destroy this place and will change the customs that Moses handed on to us." And all who sat in the council looked intently at him, and they saw that his face was like the face of an angel.
>
> —Acts 6:11-15

When asked by the high priest if the accusations were true, Stephen took the occasion to rehearse the story of Jesus, holding nothing back. The people couldn't contain their anger after hearing Stephen.

> They became enraged and ground their teeth at Stephen. But filled with the Holy Spirit, he gazed into heaven and saw the glory of God and Jesus standing at the right hand of God. "Look," he said, "I see the heavens opened and the Son of Man standing at the right hand of God!" But they covered their ears, and with a loud shout all rushed together against him.
>
> —Acts 7:54-57

Reflecting and Recording

Ponder these two stories. What are the similarities? The differences? Make some notes.

Is there any difference to your responses to the two stories? How did you respond to the first? The second? Spend a few minutes examining your responses.

■ ■ ■

Did you feel any anger in reading the stories? At what did you feel anger? Spend two or three minutes thinking about it. Record some notes.

Is there any question about anger being a deadly sin?

■ ■ ■

During the Day

Pay attention to what makes you angry today. Is it something done to you? to someone else? Is it the attitudes and actions of another? Is it because you are threatened? As you feel anger, register the feeling and ask, Why?

DAY 2

Be Angry and Sin Not

Righteous indignation. We have heard people use the term to describe their anger. We have claimed it ourselves. There certainly is such a thing. Paul cautioned the Ephesians, "Be angry but do not sin" (Eph. 4:26). That suggests that anger is not always sin. Not all anger is wrong. Here is a picture of anger as righteous indignation.

> The Passover of the Jews was near, and Jesus went up to Jerusalem. In the temple he found people selling cattle, sheep, and doves, and the money changers seated at their tables. Making a whip of cords, he drove all of them out of the temple, both the sheep and the cattle. He also poured out the coins of the money changers and overturned their tables. He told those who were selling the doves, "Take these things out of here! Stop making my Father's house a marketplace!" His disciples remembered that it was written, "Zeal for your house will consume me." The Jews then said to him, "What sign can you show us for doing this?" Jesus answered them, "Destroy this temple, and in three days I will raise it up." The Jews then said, "This temple has been under construction for forty-six years, and will you raise it up in three days?" But he was speaking of the temple of his body. After he was raised from the dead, his disciples remembered that he had said this; and they believed the scripture and the word that Jesus had spoken.
>
> —John 2:13-22

Have you ever questioned how Jesus could have done this? Using an improvised whip, driving from the Temple a dozen or more persons. How could he do it? They certainly could have kept Jesus from overturning their tables and driving out of the Temple their sheep and cattle, and loosing their doves from their cages. They were as physically strong as he and together they could have withstood his one-man effort to cleanse the Temple.

Note verse 17: "His disciples remembered that it was written, 'Zeal for your house will consume me.' " They were identifying Jesus as the Messiah. When the Jews questioned Jesus as to why he had done the Temple cleansing, Jesus responded: "Destroy this temple, and in three days I will raise it up" (John 2:19).

Jesus was speaking about his death and resurrection, and later the disciples recalled this. So how was Jesus able to run the money-changers and those who were selling cattle, sheep, and doves out of the Temple? It was not his physical strength but his moral power. The moral force of Jesus' anger against their use of the sacrificial system to take advantage of the poor sent them scrambling from the Temple. Jesus had righteousness on his side.

The lesson? Only the anger of a humble person has the moral force that can be rightly labeled "righteous indignation." Only the truly humble can be angry without sinning. Why? Because the anger is not the result of personal hurt or wounded pride. It is anger for a righteous cause, anger against that which *violates God's way* and/or *hurts others.*

- We should be angry when we discover landlords in our community charging poor people exorbitant rent for houses not fit for human habitation.
- We should be angry when our criminal justice system punishes lightly a white-collar crime involving millions of dollars but comes down oppressively on a poor person who steals clothing from a department store.
- We should express our righteous indignation against a system that allows civil servants to waste money because it is budgeted ($150 for a hammer, $30 for a screwdriver, $10 million overrides on a defense contract) while all the time reducing the support for poor children and old people.

Few of us, however, can claim that our anger is righteous indignation. It is very rare that our anger does not have our personal self-interest mixed up in it.

There is a call to be angry, but the call is kept in balance: "Be angry but do not sin." We must always seek to be sure that our anger is righteous and our indignation moral. George Matheson prayed, "O Lord, Thou knowest that I do well to be angry, but I have mistaken the times." That may be the right prayer for all of us.

Reflecting and Recording

List five situations when you have been most angry during the past month.

(1)

(2)

(3)

(4)

(5)

Now look carefully at each situation. What evoked the anger? A person? A mistake you made? Your pride was hurt? Someone spoke unkindly, accusingly, condemningly to you or of you? Someone you loved was hurt? You witnessed injustice?

■ ■ ■

Look at each of these now and ask, Was the anger justified?

■ ■ ■

Look again at each. Was any an expression of "righteous indignation"?

During the Day

Continue to pay attention to what makes you angry. As you feel anger, register the feeling and ask, Why?

DAY 3

"This Thing of Being a Man"

The size of a man can be measured by the size of the thing that makes him angry." I don't know who first said that, but Aaron Lott, the Baptist preacher to whom we were introduced on Day 1 could have said it. He certainly knew it.

His most powerful deacon, Booker Brown, tried to talk him out of challenging the Jim Crow system. Booker appealed to him to think of his family—his wife, Rachel, and his son, Jonah. Then Aaron tells Brother Booker a question that his son asked.

> "Daddy," he said, "how come you ain't a man?" I got mad, I did, and told him: "I am a man." He said that wasn't what he meant. "I mean," he said, "how come you ain't a man where white folks concerned?" I couldn't answer him, Booker. I'll never forget it till the day I die.

Then Aaron concluded by saying:

> This thing of being a man, Booker, is a big thing. The Supreme Court can't make you a man. The NAACP can't do it. God Almighty can do a lot, but even He can't do it. Ain't nobody can do it but you.
>
> —Abbott, p. 46

This thing of being a man is a big thing because "the size of a man can be measured by the size of the thing that makes him angry." Aaron was angry—angry at a system that had reduced him to less than human, that had robbed him and his people of self-esteem, dignity, and feelings of worth, and he was ready to pay the price—even to die—to challenge that sin.

Go back and read from Day 1 the passage describing the anger of Sheriff Sampson and the mob against Aaron (pages 77–78).

■ ■ ■

Spend two or three minutes pondering the difference between Aaron's anger, which gave him the courage to offer his life for a cause, and that of those who killed him.

■ ■ ■

As we considered yesterday, anger is not always a sin. We see that in the story of Aaron Lott. We need to be on guard against tolerance and apathy in the presence of evil. It is not only easy to become the victims of evil, we may even become evil's instruments. Keeping that perspective, we can focus more clearly on anger as a deadly sin.

You may have a hard time moving in your mind from the anger that stems from racial bigotry or religious prejudice that leads to the violent killing of innocent people such as Aaron Lott and the New Testament preacher Stephen to the role anger plays in our day-to-day life. Yet we need to make that transition.

It is humiliating to think of how much of our anger is sparked by trifles. Robert Burns challenged us:

> Oh wad some power the giftie gie us
> To see oursels as ithers see us!

We tense up when the driver in front of us fails to move on when the red light changes to green. We begin to seethe inside when we discover that our wife didn't pick up our clothes at the cleaner, and we wanted to wear a particular shirt. Our three-year-old overturns her glass of milk at the dinner table; our ten-year-old tracks mud onto the kitchen floor that we had mopped only an hour before. List three trifles that at least began a burn of anger in you during this past week.

(1)

(2)

(3)

These trifles are not what the deadly sin of anger is about. They simply underscore the fact that one of the first perversions of human nature to show itself is anger. Before a child can talk, he or she can express anger. Being human involves handling anger. The writer of Proverbs puts it in this perspective.

> In the transgression of the evil there is a snare, but the righteous sing and rejoice. The righteous know the rights of the poor; the wicked have no such understanding. Scoffers set a city aflame, but the wise turn away wrath. If the wise go to law with fools, there is a ranting and ridicule without relief. The bloodthirsty hate the blameless, and they seek the life of the upright. A fool gives full vent to anger, but the wise quietly holds it back.
>
> —Proverbs 29:6-11

In all of our thinking about anger and our efforts to deal with it, we must remember that it is not the impulse of anger but the way we handle it that turns into sin. Incapacity for anger is as unhealthy and dysfunctional as screaming or clenching our teeth and muttering insults, or going to bed with a sick headache.

We discussed yesterday that not to be angry at the injustice around us is to be out of touch with a huge portion of life. Anger is a normal response to personal hurt and perceived injustice. We need, then, to admit our anger and own it as inspiration and power to work at solving the problems about which we are angry.

Reflecting and Recording

Being angry at and confronting unfairness, supporting persons who are being used and made "underdogs," standing up for justice, make us feel good about ourselves. Such action enhances our self-esteem. Can you think of an occasion when this has been true in your life? Describe that experience in five or six sentences.

Are there situations of unfairness and injustice in your community about which you should be angry?

■ ■ ■

Pray this prayer attributed to Saint Francis of Assisi:
> O Lord, make me an instrument of your peace.
> Where there is hatred let me sow love;
> Where there is injury, pardon;
> Where there is doubt, faith;
> Where there is despair, hope;
> Where there is darkness, light;
> Where there is sadness, joy.

During the Day

The prayer you have just prayed is printed on page 183. Cut it out and take it with you for the next four or five days. Whenever you have a chance—waiting for an appointment or at a traffic light, during a coffee break—pray it. We hope that during these next days you will memorize it, so that you can call it to mind and pray it often.

DAY 4

Color Me Red

Stephen Shoemaker reminds us that there are two primitive Hebrew words for anger that provide picturesque meaning:

> The first word is to have "pregnant nostrils." When you act angry the nostrils enlarge. The same Hebrew word is used for nose and anger. The famous phrase describing God as "slow to anger" (Exod. 34:6) literally means to be "long of nose." The other word means "to burn" or to "grow hot." We think of anger in degrees of heat as well as tones of red. We use phrases like "boiling mad" or "hotheaded" or "flaming temper."
>
> —Shoemaker, p. 60

We say of a person, "She was red with anger." Cartoonists picture persons turning red as they get angry.

There are two kinds of anger: the blazing and the brooding, or what may be called the "powder keg" and the "Crock-Pot" kinds. *USA TODAY* once reported that a Dadeville, Alabama, man became angry because he lost a Bible-quoting contest. He shot and killed Gabel Taylor, a thirty-eight-year-old man who beat him in the contest. That's powder-keg anger—like gun powder, the least little spark ignites an explosion.

Brooding anger simmers, like the roast we cook in a Crock-Pot—slowly stewing all day long. This fuming anger often results in violence. Psychologists and psychiatrists often diagnose violent rapists and/or murderers as persons whose anger has been seething within, bottled up and smoldering until it finally erupts. It is no wonder that the Parson in *The Canterbury Tales* called anger the "Devil's furnace." Not only do we connect the color *red* with anger, we speak of a person being "purple with rage." Rage is anger out of control.

On the day-to-day level, either kind of anger may lead to sin. Explosive anger may cause a person to strike a spouse or to punish a child with physical abuse. Estimates of the number of women battered each year range from two million to four million according to Antonia C. Novello, Surgeon General of the United States (1990–93). Hundreds of women are murdered by their husbands or their boyfriends each year. Some sources indicate that ten million children receive abuse every year at the hands of members of their families.

Anger causes murder and leads to war. It provokes diabolical actions that make the headlines. But it also leads to spiteful attitudes that go unnoticed in the public eye, yet tears persons to pieces in the home and plays havoc in relationships. We will look more at brooding anger on Day 6. Focus now on blazing anger, the powder-keg kind.

Powder-keg anger, unleashed in quick flashes of violent actions or bellowing voices, is very often the shout for attention. It is anger that announces something is wrong. It is a red flag warning us to turn around before we go too far. Unless we examine ourselves and discover the source of our misery, spend our energy on the unfinished building and/or repairing of relationships, we will end up over the precipice in destructive action that can't be undone.

Because anger is such a part of being human—and what we are angry at determines the kind of person we are—three things are essential.

- We must accept and own our anger.
- We must learn to understand it.
- We must express our anger in appropriate, nondestructive, nonsinful ways.

These three essentials must be perceived in light of the teaching of scripture:

> You must understand this, my beloved: let everyone be quick to listen, slow to speak, slow to anger; for your anger does not produce God's righteousness. Therefore rid yourselves of all sordidness and rank growth of wickedness, and welcome with meekness the implanted word that has the power to save your souls.
>
> —James 1:19-21

The pivotal truth is verse 20: "Your anger does not produce God's righteousness."

Reflecting and Recording

Uninvestigated anger is a barrier to our health and wholeness as persons in relation to Christ and to others. On Day 2 you were asked to list the five occasions when you have been angry during the past month. Go back and look at that list. In a word or two identify those occasions again.

(1)

(2)

(3)

(4)

(5)

Along with those five occasions try to recall two occasions of your greatest anger and describe them briefly here.

(6)

(7)

Look now at each of these and identify your anger as blazing (powder keg) or brooding (Crock Pot). Label each of them.

■ ■ ■

Now look again at your list. Does any occasion of anger indicate a strained or broken relationship?

■ ■ ■

Look again at your list. Do any of the occasions of anger indicate stress in your work?

■ ■ ■

Read the list again. Was any of your anger provoked by the unfairness of life (a loved one died; someone else got the promotion or job you wanted; a child was born with a handicapping condition; you are an alcoholic while others can drink without seeming harm or addiction)?

■ ■ ■

Do any of the suggestions of why you may have been angry suggest occasions of anger that you haven't thought of before? If so, make notes to describe them here.

During the Day

When you feel anger coming on, stop and ask yourself, *What is this telling me about myself and what is going on in my life?*

DAY 5

Anger with Self, Anger with God

The LORD is gracious and merciful, slow to anger and abounding in steadfast love. The LORD is good to all, and his compassion is over all that he has made. . . . The LORD upholds all who are falling, and raises up all who are bowed down. The eyes of all look to you, and you give them their food in due season. You open your hand, satisfying the desire of every living thing. The LORD is just in all his ways, and kind in all his doings. The LORD is near to all who call on him, to all who call on him in truth. He fulfills the desire of all who fear him; he also hears their cry, and saves them.

—Psalm 145:8-9, 14-19

Spend a minute or two reflecting on this word. Can you affirm the conviction of the psalmist—that God is gracious, generous, and good?

■ ■ ■

Yesterday in your Reflecting and Recording you were asked to explore whether any of your anger came from the unfairness of life. That was a deliberate choice of words. The way many would state it is the "unfairness of God." That's the reason many people feel anger toward God. They think God is unfair. God did not grant them what they asked in prayer.

There are also people who are angry with themselves. We have a friend who is a very successful businessman. He has amassed a fortune and his family has had an overabundance of material things. Unhappiness abounds in that family. His daughter has been divorced twice, though she is only twenty-nine. His son dropped out of college and now, at age thirty-two, moves from one job to another, surviving but without meaning, never married and in and out of relationships, dependent on drugs and alcohol. The father is angry with himself because he blames himself for his children's failures. He was not available as a father when his children needed him most.

It is healthy for this father to acknowledge his failure and to do everything possible to build a relationship, to love and support his children where they are now. But it is destructive for him to be angry with himself, to continue to emotionally lacerate himself and find ways to punish himself for his failure.

Wanting revenge is an expression of anger. We need to realize that this vengeful attitude can be addressed to self as well as to others. If we are angry with ourselves, it may very well be that we will seek to punish ourselves even as we would seek to get revenge against others who have made us angry.

The perspective we need is, *Life isn't fair, but life isn't God.* There is mystery here and we will never be able to fathom or explain evil. Why the rains fall on the just and the unjust will remain a philosophical problem. Why we don't come to our senses and to maturity before we damage the lives of those around us is a puzzle, but also a sure sign of original sin.

We don't have to be in bondage either to the mystery of life-isn't-fair or to our sinful nature. To be angry with God and with ourselves is a sign of our bondage. The revenge that flows from anger expresses our refusal to trust the love, righteousness, and final justice of God.

The deadly sin of anger denies the love and justice of God. In our vengeful anger we put ourselves in God's place, becoming the judge rather than leaving that to God. Paul warned against our vengeful actions, and closed his argument with these words:

> Beloved, never avenge yourselves, but leave room for the wrath of God; for it is written, "Vengeance is mine, I will repay, says the Lord." No, "if your enemies are hungry, feed them; if they are thirsty, give them something to drink; for by doing this you will heap burning coals on their heads." Do not be overcome by evil, but overcome evil with good.
>
> —Romans 12:19-21

Reflecting and Recording

Can you remember an occasion when you were angry and sought to get revenge? Describe that experience here.

In seeking revenge, what happened to you and the person against whom you were vengeful? Describe the results here.

Describe the last time you were angry with God. (Don't pass this off quickly. Take some time and be honest. Describe the experience.)

Spend whatever time you can reflecting on this assertion: *Life isn't fair, but life isn't God.*

■ ■ ■

During the Day

You have been praying a prayer attributed to Saint Francis of Assisi. You know now the first petition, "Lord, make me an instrument of your peace." When you are prone to anger today, make that petition and seek ways to offer God's peace to others.

DAY 6

Making Room for the Devil

Now this I affirm and insist on in the Lord: you must no longer live as the Gentiles live, in the futility of their minds. They are darkened in their understanding, alienated from the life of God because of their ignorance and hardness of heart. They have lost all sensitivity and have abandoned themselves to licentiousness, greedy to practice every kind of impurity. This is not the way you learned Christ! For surely you have heard about him and were taught in him, as truth is in Jesus. You were taught to put away your former way of life, your old self, corrupt and deluded by its lusts, and to be renewed in the spirit of your minds, and to clothe yourselves with the new self, created according to the likeness of God in true righteousness and holiness. So then, putting away falsehood, let all of us speak the truth to our neighbors, for we are members of one another. Be angry but do not sin; do not let the sun go down on your anger, and do not make room for the devil. Thieves must give up stealing; rather let them labor and work honestly with their own hands, so as to have something to share with the needy. Let no evil talk come out of your mouths, but only what is useful for building up, as there is need, so that your words may give grace to those who hear.

—Ephesians 4:17-29

This passage is set in the context of Paul's calling Christians to live or walk as new persons. The word *walk* is an action word, encompassing the whole of our lives, the way we think and relate, behave and respond—the way we act publicly as well as the way we appear to others. The walk of a Christian is Paul's way of talking about the daily conduct, the morality, the distinctive marks of those who are seeking Christian maturity.

As mentioned earlier, the Bible does not specifically catalog the seven deadly sins, yet all of them are addressed frequently. In the above passage and in the balance of chapters 4 and 5 of Ephesians, Paul comes close to a listing. He specifically names greed, lust, avarice, hardness of heart, and pride ("darkened in their understanding"). He extensively catalogs debauched and evil attitudes and actions that must be put away from the Christian life. He paints a vivid picture: "They have lost all sensitivity and have abandoned themselves to licentiousness, greedy to practice every kind of impurity" (Eph. 4:19).

In this setting, which is Paul's description of people living in the futility of their minds, darkened in their understanding, and alienated from the life of God, he talks about anger: "Be angry but do not sin; do not let the sun go down on your anger" (v. 26). Then immediately comes this word: "Do not make room for the devil" (v. 27).

Paul knew that the devil is real. The devil wants to control our lives. His most malicious trick is to convince us that he is not real, that he does not exist. If he can convince us of that, warnings like that of Paul ("do not make room for the devil") won't mean anything. Giving in to the practicing of the seven deadly sins—or any other sin—is making room for the devil.

This is certainly the case with anger—and especially the brooding, Crock-Pot kind. As anger seethes and smolders, as we repress it, refuse to accept and own it, fail to express it in appropriate nondestructive, nonsinful ways, we make room for the devil. We invite

- resentment that leads us to self-hate and hatred of others;
- bitterness that mushrooms as it feeds on the real and/or imagined wrongs done to us;
- malignant grudges that destroy *us*, not the one against whom we have the grudges;
- hostility that makes us suspicious of the motives of others, turns others into enemies, and makes us defensive in our reactions and responses.

All of these destructive forces and more are the result of unresolved anger. The devil can have a heyday with any of these as his weapon.

"James Joyce's portrait of a clergyman has a devastating fitness: The face was eyeless and sour-favored and devout, shot through with pink tinges of suffocated anger" (Olsson, p. 30). The description is not isolated to the one preacher; it has a devastating fitness for us who allow anger to brood in the darkness of unowned, unacknowledged, unexpressed feelings fed by the illusions of our own goodness and our distorted notions about life treating us unfairly.

"The punishment of the angry in *The Divine Comedy* is to be enveloped in suffocating smoke" (Olsson, p. 30). We know something about that. It is not the raging conflagrations of anger like blowing up the Alfred P. Murrah Federal Building in Oklahoma City, but the low-burn "trifling angers" such as we discussed on Day 3 that suffocate most of our lives. Olsson paints a picture of one aspect of it.

"Suffocated anger"—there's your bull's eye. That's the mark of the moralist—the man trying to be good all by himself. It ought not be the portrait of the Christian. Or is it true that we also live in the illusion of our own goodness?

So that we cannot face our failures but stuff them like wet clouts into the half-forgotten things of the mind, the way we try to burn wet garbage in the kitchen stove that will not draw. And out of our failures and our irritations there eventually arises a damp and sourish smoke which befogs our life and makes everything look wrong to us. Because we did not localize the blame in ourselves and have it burned away into the hot fire of grace, we must now ascribe our misery to some sort of universal conspiracy. And end by yipping and snarling at things like ill-tempered dogs.

—Olsson, pp. 30–31

Reflecting and Recording

The following is a list of what happens when we make room for the devil by failing to accept, acknowledge, and deal with our anger. If any of these are present in your life, acknowledge them by making some notes about what is going on, the circumstances and people involved, and how you are being affected by it.

(1) Resentment that leads to self-hate and hatred of others:

(2) Bitterness that mushrooms as it feeds on the real and/or imagined wrongs done to us:

(3) Malignant grudges that destroy us, not the one against whom we have the grudges:

(4) Hostility that makes us suspicious of the motives of others, turns others into enemies, and makes us defensive in our reaction and responses:

Look now at the expressions of suppressed anger which you have acknowledged above. Turn your acknowledgment of the presence of anger into a prayer of confession to the Lord. Write your prayer here.

Look now at what you have confessed. Do you need to share any of this with some other person? Do you need to ask forgiveness of someone? Is there a relationship to which you need to give special attention in communication and efforts at reconciliation?

■ ■ ■

During the Day

Begin to do some of the things that in your above reflection you felt you need to do.

DAY 7

Invitation and Imperative

Therefore be imitators of God, as beloved children, and live in love, as Christ loved us and gave himself up for us, a fragrant offering and sacrifice to God. But fornication and impurity of any kind, or greed, must not even be mentioned among you, as is proper among saints. Entirely out of place is obscene, silly, and vulgar talk; but instead, let there be thanksgiving. Be sure of this, that no fornicator or impure person, or one who is greedy (that is, an idolater), has any inheritance in the kingdom of Christ and of God. Let no one deceive you with empty words, for because of these things the wrath of God comes on those who are disobedient. Therefore do not be associated with them. For once you were darkness, but now in the Lord you are light. Live as children of light—for the fruit of the light is found in all that is good and right and true. Try to find out what is pleasing to the Lord. Take no part in the unfruitful works of darkness, but instead expose them.

—Ephesians 5:1-11

On Day 7 of Week One, we discussed that we can't give our sins to Jesus; rather we give ourselves to Jesus and he takes our sin from us and gives us the power to overcome sin's grip. The gospel is always an invitation and an imperative: You are a child of God; now become a child of God. You are a new person in Christ; grow up into that new person. So Paul could say, "Now in the Lord you are light. Live as children of light."

The walk of a Christian is a walk of grace—receiving the pardon and power of Christ—and a walk of discipline—exercising our will and energy to be "imitators" of Christ and to live in love. This is the way we deal with all the deadly sins.

With anger, there are four areas of discipline to which we must give our attention. The first is *hanging on*. We can never get over or past repressed anger if we want to hang on to it.

Our wounds do not heal if we continually pick at the scabs. We may intellectually decide that we will not be angry anymore, but if something in us wants to nurture the resentment and bitterness, then we will remain in its clutches. In his poem "Tam o' Shanter" Robert Burns describes a woman waiting for her husband to come home from the pub. She was "nursing her wrath to keep it warm." We must deliberately, in an act of will and in the power Christ provides, honestly confront our repressed anger, our resentment and bitterness. It may be an issue with parenting, a hurt we received from a child or spouse, a situation at work, an insult or injury received months, even years, ago. What do we need to do or to say in order to cease hanging on? Not to act will create more bitterness, more resentment, more self-loathing.

The second area of discipline in relation to anger has to do with *list keeping*. In *Believing in Myself*, Ernie Larson and Carol Hegarty have said it well: "The problem is that list making keeps us fixated at the point of our losses. It nails us to the past, forever victimized, forever on the lookout for more of the same."

The third area of discipline is *revealing our anger to others*. It is easy to get locked up in anger—hostile thinking patterns and resentment which run us around in circles. Carrying a grudge, or giving mental hospitality to the desire for revenge are cancers inside us. As long as we keep these feelings and thoughts to ourselves, we recycle the same blind and misguided approach to life. We break out of this negative cycle by revealing our anger to others. Naming and verbalizing reduces our anger and/or causes of its power over us. Receiving acceptance, perspective, and feedback from others enables us to think clearly and act decisively.

The fourth area of discipline is *forgiveness*. Forgiveness and anger cannot live together. You cannot be resentful and forgiving at the same time. They are like fire and water. The water will either put the fire out or the fire will vaporize the water. Whichever is greater—anger or forgiveness—will prevail.

When Jesus died on the cross, paying the price for our sins, he said, "It is finished" (John 19:30). The only way we can discipline ourselves to forgive is to accept completely what Christ has done for us and remember Christ's sacrificial love when we need to forgive others. Jesus does not make us pay. How then can we harbor resentment for and desire revenge against others? If we retain a vision of Christ hanging on the cross, saying, "It is finished," when our anger boils and vengeful thoughts come, we can forgive and it will be finished. We won't hang on to it, harbor and nurture it, make our lists and fixate on our hurt. Jesus didn't make us pay. Dare we think we should make others pay? We will never be free of any anger or pain or resentment brought on us by others until in the deep recesses of our hearts we have forgiveness.

Reflecting and Recording

Examine your life. Is there pain and resentment that, for some unexplained or unknown reason, you are hanging on to?

■ ■ ■

Are you a list keeper? Do you seek to justify your anger and resentment by remembering all the things someone has done that were disrespectful, hurtful, sarcastic—all that which diminished your feeling of worth?

■ ■ ■

Is there some grudge, some resentment, some seething anger which you need to get out in the open by sharing with another?

■ ■ ■

List the last three times that you have been hurt the most.

(1)

(2)

(3)

Are you still angry about any of these? Are you still feeling pain? resentment? bitterness?

■ ■ ■

Are there persons related to your past hurt that you need to forgive? Name those persons here.

Now spend as much time as needed praying for those persons and for the strength of will to forgive them.

During the Day

Write a letter, go see, or call on the phone the persons you listed above and let them know you forgive them.

Group Meeting for Week Four

Note: The leader for this week should bring a whiteboard or newsprint to the group meeting. (See suggestion number 1 of Sharing Together below.)

Introduction

Most of us have yet to see the dynamic potential of the conversation which takes place in an intentional group such as this. Life is found in communion with God and also in conversation with others.

Speaking and listening with this sort of deep meaning which communicates life is not easy. This week our emphasis has been on anger. We are fully aware by now that sharing personally about the deadly sins is not easy. All of us have deep experiences not easy to talk about. Therefore, listening and responding to what we hear is very important. To really hear another person helps him or her to think clearly and gain perspective. It may contribute to the healing process. To listen, then, is an act of love. When we listen in a way that makes a difference, we surrender ourselves to the other person, saying, "I will hear what you have to say and will receive you as I receive your words." When we speak in a way that makes a difference, we speak for the sake of others; thus we are contributing to the wholeness process.

Sharing Together

1.   Ask the group to turn to page 81 of their workbooks where they listed the five occasions when they have been most angry during the past month. Invite each person to share at least one occasion of anger. Have someone act as a "scribe" to record these on whiteboard or newsprint as they are shared. Write just enough to be clear. Do that now.
      A.   Look at the list now. Discuss what evoked the anger. Put a yes or no beside each as you decide whether the anger was justified or not.
      B.   Now look at the list. Put a check by each one that could be considered righteous indignation.
2.   Continue, if you feel a need to do so, in discussing anger as righteous indignation and when anger is healthy.
3.   Read the list of "anger for a righteous cause" on page 80. Looking at your own community, record on the whiteboard or newsprint things about which you should be angry. Is any person in the group taking action in relation to these issues?
4.   Invite the group to call to mind their responses to the two stories on Day 1: Pastor Aaron Lott and Stephen the martyr. Spend ten or fifteen minutes discussing the kind of anger persons felt in reading the stories—also, their responses to the anger in the stories.
5.   Though it may be difficult to make the transition, spend four to six minutes talking about how much of our anger is sparked by trifles. A good way to start is to invite each person to name the common things that make them most angry.
6.   Invite any persons who will to share an experience when they were angry at the unfairness of life or angry with God.
7.   Now invite any persons who will to share an experience of being angry with themselves.
8.   Against the backdrop of this sharing, spend five to ten minutes talking about the perspective that life isn't fair, but life isn't God.
9.   Is there a person in the group who would share an experience of anger that led to seeking revenge and what happened?
10.   Spend the balance of your sharing time talking about the four expressions of and/or responses to anger about which we must discipline ourselves (Day 7): hanging on, list keeping, revealing our anger to others, and forgiveness.

Praying Together

Corporate prayer is one of the great blessings of Christian community. To affirm that is one thing; to experience it is another. To experience it we have to experiment with the possibility.

Will you become a bit bolder now, and experiment with the possibilities of corporate prayer by sharing more openly and intimately?

1. Begin your prayer time by turning to page 92 of your workbook where ways that we make room for the devil are listed. The leader will read the list and pause after each. At the pause, if you identify with what is stated, say aloud, "Guilty."

2. Move into silence now. Spend three to five minutes in quietness, asking and answering these two questions: Is there a specific need for forgiveness in my life? Is there resentment or bitterness which I need to confess?

3. Let each person who will share his/her need for forgiveness and/or the confession of resentment or bitterness. As this is done, other persons in the group may find it helpful to take notes on this sharing so all can pray in a more centered way.

4. There is a sense in which, through this sharing, you have already been corporately praying. There is power, however, in a community on a common journey verbalizing thoughts and feelings to God in the presence of fellow pilgrims. Experiment with this possibility now.

    A. Let the leader call each person's name, pausing briefly after each name for some person in the group to offer a brief verbal prayer focused on what that person has shared. It could be as simple as "Lord, give Jane the confidence that she is forgiven," or "Loving God, give John the sense of your healing power in his struggle with his resentment against _____." (Leader, remember to call your own name.)

    B. When all names have been called and all persons prayed for, sit in silence for two minutes; be open to the strength of love that is yours in community. Enjoy being linked with persons who are mutually concerned.

Week Five

Sloth
Not Caring

DAY 1

Laziness—A Sin?

In the modern vernacular, sloth is laziness. Who would claim that laziness is a virtue? But can we go so far as to think of it as a sin? A human weakness? Yes. A character defect? Maybe. But who would list it as a major sin?

Scripture does. And of course the church fathers cataloged it as one of the seven deadly sins. The book of Proverbs is especially tough on lazy persons, sparing no images in describing laziness, and expressing in colorful language the destructiveness of it.

> Go to the ant, you lazybones; consider its ways, and be wise. Without having any chief
> or officer or ruler, it prepares its food in summer, and gathers its sustenance in harvest.
> How long will you lie there, O lazybones? When will you rise from your sleep? A little
> sleep, a little slumber, a little folding of the hands to rest, and poverty will come upon
> you like a robber, and want, like an armed warrior.
>
> —Proverbs 6:6-11

M. Scott Peck, a psychiatrist and a Christian who has written some of the most helpful and popular books in psychotherapy, says that laziness is a major cause of evil and a primary source of psychological illness. He sees laziness as the main reason we Americans are failing at human relations. Even at the most surface level, it takes effort to enter into and maintain human relationships. Stop for a moment now and consider the thought that *laziness prevents us from loving.*

■ ■ ■

If laziness prevents us from loving, then laziness is certainly a sin. Laziness is a sin because it poisons the will. This is the way I once reflected on it in a sixty-second radio-television commentary called *Perceptions* that presented observations on everyday life:

- When the death of Calvin Coolidge was made public, someone quipped, "But how can they tell?"
- George Bernard Shaw once said that the epitaph for many people should read, "Died at 30; buried at 60."

- You're dead when the suffering of another causes you no pain.
- You're dead when your blood does not run hot in the face of blatant injustice.
- You're dead when you evade truth that hurts and accept an easy lie.
- You're dead when you are not willing to put forth the energy necessary to save a dying relationship.

—*Perceptions*, p. 57

Is that a picture of laziness?

Reflecting and Recording

Spend a few minutes reflecting on laziness as you have seen it in yourself and in others.

■ ■ ■

Write a definition of laziness.

Spend a few minutes reflecting on how laziness becomes a sin by poisoning the will.

■ ■ ■

During the Day

As you move through the day, guard against laziness preventing you from expressing love. Note that sometimes you may be weary and tired—but don't let that prevent you from acting in a loving way.

DAY 2

The Sweet Doing of Nothing

Stephen Shoemaker reminds us, "The Italians have a phrase *dulce far niente* which translates 'the sweet doing of nothing.' We will find ourselves resisting consideration of laziness as a sin unless we admit at the beginning that there is a difference between laziness and restfulness. In the hurried, harried world in which we live, restfulness may be, at times at least, a very healthy necessity. Inactivity may sometimes be our most needed spiritual activity.

So, let us affirm that idleness, which is often seen as sloth or laziness, is not only acceptable, in many of us it needs cultivating. Type A personalities, such as we, often become workaholics. It is easy for us to become too absorbed in what we are doing, too heavily earnest, too seriously involved. We become so driven that we don't live, we are lived—our jobs, our involvements, determine our lives. Those who are mercilessly driven by a rigid "Puritan" work ethic, and who pressure others to fit their pattern, need to learn to appreciate a life rhythm that includes "doing nothing."

Psalm 46 is a psalm we need to read often. It will help us get what we are doing and/or failing to do in perspective. Here are portions of it.

> God is our refuge and strength, a very present help in trouble. Therefore we will not fear, though the earth should change, though the mountains shake in the heart of the sea; though its waters roar and foam, though the mountains tremble with its tumult. There is a river whose streams make glad the city of God, the holy habitation of the Most High. God is in the midst of the city; it shall not be moved; God will help it when the morning dawns. The nations are in an uproar, the kingdoms totter; he utters his voice, the earth melts. . . . "Be still, and know that I am God! I am exalted among the nations. I am exalted in the earth." The LORD of hosts is with us; the God of Jacob is our refuge.
>
> —Psalm 46:1-6; 10-11

The root word for *mystery* is a Greek word meaning literally "to shut one's mouth." The psalmist was thinking in those terms. "Be still, and know that I am God!" Our friend Tom Trotter, a leader in theological education, reminded us once that this word, often uttered in breathless tones, is a shout. It means, "Shut up! while I tell it like it is." We need that kind of disengagement.

So we urge you not to be defensive during these days as we explore the sin of sloth. Keep perspective and know that when we talk about sloth we are not talking about lingering long over lunch with a friend, or strolling aimlessly through the woods with a person you love, or spending a day doing nothing because the demands of your job are about to do you in, or moving through a weekend without the fret of hurry, purpose, or chore, or "wasting" an hour watching a sunset or listening to the sounds of nature, or spending whatever time alone in silence to quiet your spirit and get back in tune with God.

As we reflected yesterday, the real root of sloth and that which makes it sinful lies in the will. The will is the executive part—the active decision-making part of our nature. Sloth is an infectious disease which poisons the will. Left to its insidious working, it will spread and become more intense, until it paralyzes and numbs the will, until any "extra" effort or demand of energy, no matter what the cause, "just isn't worth it."

When we were growing up in rural Mississippi, fishing was our favorite pastime, especially in the summer. Our fishing was not fancy—no rod and reels, or fly-casting, just a cane pole, a line, a sinker, a hook, and of course, a cork. The cork would float in the water wherever the stream took it. When it bobbled, we knew we were getting a nibble; when it sank we knew we had a good bite and we needed to set the hook and land the fish.

We are not to live life as corks, floating aimlessly, being taken wherever the current chooses. Under God's guidance and with God's support, we are to choose direction, take control, and, by the decisions and disciplines of our will, determine where we go. We must use our wills in redirecting our type A drivenness and choose to be idle and do nothing when that is necessary. We must also be vigilant against laziness which poisons the will.

Reflecting and Recording

Look at the ways you have failed in exercising your will. Make some notes on the time you failed to be idle, to do nothing in a positive way for the good of your soul. Be specific.

Now make some notes about any danger sign you see that your will may be infected with sloth. Are you finding yourself caring less? less excited about giving of your time and energy?

During the Day

Continue to guard against laziness preventing you from expressing love. But also be attentive to whether your overactivity is preventing you from getting the rest and renewal you need.

DAY 3

Preventing Loving

On Day 1 we considered the fact that laziness is a sin because it poisons the will. For that reason, laziness prevents us from loving. This assertion calls for a consideration of the role feelings and will play in love.

Unfortunately, most of us think love is something we feel rather than something we do. How many times have you heard it? "When you fall in love, you will know it." How many times have you said it? "Don't worry; you will feel it." We reduce love to how we feel about someone. Jesus would not agree with us.

> As the Father has loved me, so I have loved you; abide in my love. If you keep my commandments, you will abide in my love, just as I have kept my Father's commandments and abide in his love. I have said these things to you so that my joy may be in you, and that your joy may be complete. This is my commandment, that you love one another as I have loved you. No one has greater love than this, to lay down one's life for one's friends.
>
> —John 15:9-13

You may protest, "Jesus is talking about the whole of the Christian life, not about our being in love with a person—not about the love that leads to marriage and/or keeps us in a marriage." You are right only in part. Do you see the distortion and the big mistake? We apply to marriage, the most important relationship of our life, an understanding of love that makes it far less than the love Jesus calls for in all relationships.

Paul sought to correct that superficial understanding: "Husbands, love your wives, just as Christ loved the church and gave himself up for her" (Eph. 5:25). That kind of love is certainly not dependent on feelings. I agree with M. Scott Peck that laziness prevents us from loving. Loving requires decision; it's a matter of the will. We decide to love. If love were a feeling, we could not be commanded to love. To the degree that my feelings may be controlled, only I can do it. You can't tell me how I am to feel. So, if love were feeling, Jesus couldn't command us to love.

In our counseling as pastors, we have discovered that laziness is one of the biggest factors in marriage breakups. One or both persons in the marriage is too lazy to love, too lazy to make the commitment and spend the energy required for loving.

Persons contemplating divorce will say, "There's just no love there. . . . The feelings are gone. . . . This marriage is just not what I want or think it should be. . . . The life has gone out of our relationship." The prescription for that state of relationship is simple and guarantees a high level of cure: love as an act of the will. Decide to love and start acting as though you "feel" love. Do those things that would express your love if you were "in love."

We've seen divorce abandoned and marriages restored by couples who were willing to give this prescription a legitimate effort. In fact, we've never seen it fail when both persons genuinely committed themselves to the process.

But tragically we have seen scores of couples move on to the divorce courts because they were too lazy to do the essential work. Many times they have admitted it: "I don't have the energy. I'm not sure it is worth the effort."

What we too often miss is the fact that just as how we feel influences what we do and how we act, likewise what we do and how we act influence how we feel.

Reflecting and Recording

Take a clear look at the past two months of your life. Can you identify occasions when your laziness prevented expressions of love? List up to three such occasions here, with a brief, descriptive word.

(1)

(2)

(3)

Look at your whole life now. Has there been a relationship seriously damaged or destroyed—husband/wife; parent/child; intimate friendship—because of your or the other person's unwillingness to love as an act of the will, as a commitment to caring? Write enough about that experience to get it clearly in your mind and recapture how it happened.

During the Day

If there is someone from whom you need to ask forgiveness for your lack of loving, do that today—a letter, a telephone call, or perhaps a personal visit soon.

DAY 4

Sloth: Avoiding Responsibility

Yesterday we sought to make the case that love is a matter of the will. Feelings are involved, but when we reduce love to feelings only we completely distort the heart of marriage, family, and human relationships. Love is the essence of the Judeo-Christian tradition and is at the heart of the Christian gospel. Jesus' call for us to love was not a call to conjure up warm positive feelings but a call to act with care and compassion toward those around us . . . even when we don't feel like it!

We closed our discussion yesterday by acknowledging that how we feel influences how we act, but also contending that how we act influences how we feel. Laziness is a deadly sin because it prevents action that could flavor our entire lives with meaning and transform us into Christlike persons.

In his book *On Not Leaving It to the Snake*, Harvey G. Cox suggested that the Fall might have had to do with sloth as well as pride. Adam and Eve refused to take responsibility, blaming everything on the serpent. They chose to stay on the animal level rather than assume their position and calling as children of God. There are a number of graphic pictures of the irresponsibility of laziness in the book of Proverbs. One is set in a vineyard:

> I passed by the field of one who was lazy, by the vineyard of a stupid person; and see, it was all overgrown with thorns; the ground was covered with nettles, and its stone wall was broken down. Then I saw and considered it; I looked and received instruction. A little sleep, a little slumber, a little folding of the hands to rest, and poverty will come upon you like a robber, and want, like an armed warrior.
>
> —Proverbs 24:30-34

There is a sense in which pride and sloth represent opposite sins—both deadly. "Pride is the attempt to be more than human; sloth is the attempt to be less than human. Pride seeks God's throne; sloth runs from the Garden. Pride takes on God's role; sloth escapes human responsibility." (Shoemaker, p. 42) This dimension of sloth is intimately connected with affluence. Where there is abundance, people tend not simply to satisfy their needs but to satiate themselves. This leads to gluttony, another deadly sin. One glaring sign of sloth is drug abuse among the successful and wealthy. It's an ironic twist that both persons economically and culturally deprived, and persons who have far more than plenty become victims of sloth. In their apathy, they turn to drugs and drink, and all sorts of frivolous amusement. "So what?" "What the hell?" "Oh, yeah!" become the verbal expressions of apathy getting its hold on a person's life.

Henry Fairlie sees complacency as the deadliest contemporary expression of the sin of sloth. It is connected with a brand of individualism that dominates present Western society. The most monstrous falsehood of this life-approach is the belief that I can find fulfillment and salvation in my own self. There is no community obligation. That we are "members one of another" as Christianity claims is denied. So there is no sense of responsibility. That is sin! It is deadly sin for the essence of identity is in our relationship with others. The psychoanalyst Karen Horney says we run toward others, run against them, or run away from them. Sloth is complacency that runs away from others.

Dorothy L. Sayers wrote, "The devilish strategy of Pride is that it attacks us not on our weak points, but on our strong." *(The Other Six Deadly Sins: Creed or Chaos)* Sloth pulls a reverse and attacks our weak points. It prevents us from going "out on a limb" in the support of a good cause. It won't allow us to run risks; the demands and the costs are too great. It makes us self-protective, fearful of any expression of emotion or show of vulnerability.

We said earlier that the deadly sins are interlocked. We see this with pride and sloth. Pride leads to an idolatry of self by self-assertion. Sloth leads to an idolatry of self by self-debasement and self-protection. In either case, we are looking out for Number One. And Jesus offers the saving answer for both sins: "If anyone would come after me, let him deny himself, take up his cross daily and follow me" (Luke 9:23, AP).

Reflecting and Recording

The proverb says, "A little sleep, a little slumber, a little folding of the hands to rest, and poverty will come upon you like a robber, and want, like an armed warrior" (Prov. 6:10-11). With this vivid picture in mind, spend a few minutes considering the assertion that *sloth (laziness) is the attempt to be less than human.*

■ ■ ■

Can you think of a person whose laziness has made him/her "less than human"? Briefly describe that person.

Spend two or three minutes considering this assertion: *Sloth (laziness) seeks to escape human responsibility.*

■ ■ ■

How do you respond to our suggestion that this aspect of sloth is connected with affluence?

■ ■ ■

How does your description of the person whose laziness has made him/her less than human fit with what seems to be an opposite thought—that some expressions of sloth are connected with affluence?

■ ■ ■

Spend the balance of your time reflecting on these two sentences: Pride leads to an idolatry of self by self-assertion. Sloth leads to an idolatry of self by self-debasement and self-protection.

■ ■ ■

During the Day

Pay attention to the persons you meet today. See if you identify the idolatry of self-assertion and/or the idolatry of self-debasement and self-protection.

DAY 5

"It Doesn't Matter"

*E*nnui is a French word that means boredom. This word conveys a state of weariness or dissatisfaction with life. As such, *ennui* can be used as an expression of sloth. Also, the Greek word for sloth is *acedia*, literally meaning "no care"; thus, sloth can be the reflection and living out of "It doesn't matter."

Slothful persons rationalize within themselves and with others if need be—but life remains prone, immobile, ineffective, because "it doesn't matter." There is "no care." Dorothy L. Sayers describes it in its full chilling dimension. Sloth emerges full-bloom:

> In the world it calls itself Tolerance; but in hell it is called Despair. It is the accomplice of the other sins and their worst punishment. It is the sin which believes in nothing, cares for nothing, seeks to know nothing, interferes with nothing, enjoys nothing, loves nothing, hates nothing, finds purpose in nothing, lives for nothing, and only remains alive because there is nothing it would die for.
>
> —Sayers, p. 81

Such a scathing description should at least call us to self-examination of every dimension of life where caring is called for. Look at your family. Do family members genuinely care for one another?

■ ■ ■

Is there a member of the family who demands more time and attention than the rest? How do you feel about that?

■ ■ ■

Are you overly protective of your resources of time and energy in relation to family members?

■ ■ ■

Many family counselors assert that one of the primary reasons children grow up undisciplined is because parents are too lazy to do the hard work, to invest the time and energy to teach and nurture the children in responsible living. Whether it be through looking at past failures with now adult children or in presently facing the challenge of parenting young children, we have both experienced this to be true.

Look at your community. Do the public schools need more volunteer help from parents, grandparents, and other concerned persons?

■ ■ ■

Spend a few minutes reflecting on each of the following questions.

Are there hungry people in your community? Who is paying attention to them?

Are there new people moving into your community? If so, who is making them welcome?

Are there homeless folks? Where do they stay when it is cold? How do they find food? Is there something you could do if you cared?

Do you know persons who do not know Christ and his saving grace? who do not know the gracious hospitality of a Christian community? who may not have heard the gospel of love, and/ or seen that love operative in persons who call themselves Christians?

■ ■ ■

Jesus told how it would be at the final judgment with people who lived as if "It doesn't matter"— the slothful. The basis for judgment to eternal punishment is ominously stated in the second half of the story:

> Then he will say to those at his left hand, "You that are accursed, depart from me into the eternal fire prepared for the devil and his angels; for I was hungry and you gave me no food, I was thirsty and you gave me nothing to drink, I was a stranger and you did not welcome me, naked and you did not give me clothing, sick and in prison and you did not visit me." Then they also will answer, "Lord, when was it that we saw you hungry or thirsty or a stranger or naked or sick or in prison, and did not take care of you?" Then he will answer them, "Truly I tell you, just as you did not do it to one of

the least of these, you did not do it to me." And these will go away into eternal punishment, but the righteous into eternal life.

—Matthew 25:41-46

Reflecting and Recording

Throughout this session, you were guided to stop and ponder questions related to your family and your community. Look back over the matters highlighted in relation to family and write a few sentences in response to this question: How do I need to change in relation to my family and/or particular members of it?

Now look at community concerns. There may be issues in your community more critical than the few mentioned. Think about it and write a few sentences in response to this question: How do I need to change in my involvement or lack of involvement in my community?

During the Day

Pay close attention to how you move through the day. Are you overprotective of yourself in relationships? Are you jealous of your time, irritated when someone demands time of you? Do you feel that someone is "invading your space"? Does anything you do reflect the attitude and actions of "no care"?

DAY 6

Forever Spectators

In his book *Fatal Attractions*, William R. White uses the metaphor "forever spectators" in his discussion of sloth. He begins with a story from Eli Wiesel's largely autobiographical novel, *The Town Beyond the Wall*.

> Michael, a young Jew who survived the Holocaust, traveled at great personal risk behind the Iron Curtain to his Hungarian hometown. Though his memory burned with images of the soldiers and police who had brutalized him and those he loved, Michael returned to satisfy his curiosity, not for revenge.
>
> In a strange way he understood the brutality of the executioners and the prison guards. What he did not understand was the man who lived across from the synagogue, the man who peered through his window day after day as thousands of Jews were herded into the death trains, reflecting "no pity, no pleasure, no shock, not even anger or interest. Impassive, cold, impersonal."
>
> There is a bond, Michael thought, between the brutal executioner and the victim, even though the bond is negative. "They at least belong to the same universe. But not so the spectator. The spectator is entirely beyond us, seeing without being seen, present but unnoticed."
>
> He concludes, "To be indifferent—for whatever reason—is to deny not only the validity of existence, but also its beauty. Betray, and you are a man; torture your neighbor; you're still a man. Evil is human, weakness is human; indifference is not."
>
> —White, pp. 41–42

White's word is powerful, but is he right? "Evil is human, weakness is human; indifference is not." Indifference does deny the validity of human existence; but how many of us who claim to be human are indifferent? Indifference is a deadly sin.

The primary need for human fulfillment and wholeness, for realizing the potential of being human, is love. Love is the essence of the gospel and the crown jewel of Christian character. In common thought, hate is the opposite of love. But when we think more deeply, we believe the opposite of love is not hate but apathy. With hate, there is emotion and feeling—an active response to another. The other is actually affirmed as being there.

With apathy, there is no emotion, no feeling for the other. It does not even account for the other's existence. Apathy disconnects us from the human family. This attitude can fester to the degree that it becomes the destructive sin of indifference. One sad expression of it is the national story of a woman who jumped to her death in Detroit. Television stations and newspapers across the country reported the story of several men, one carrying a crowbar, who beat the woman and chased her until she jumped to her death off a bridge over the Detroit River. Dozens of people watched; some even cheered. What was the victim's offense? Her car had crashed into a car driven by one of the men.

Some even cheered. How does one account for such indifference, such nonfeeling? Have you seen it? We have, and we have been guilty of it. Not murder, but the smashing of a dream, the choking of an idea, the crushing of enthusiasm, the putting down of a person that made him or her less than alive and whole.

How did we do it? By our inattention, our failure to listen. By our neglect in caring enough to affirm and encourage.

It's possible. We can be guilty of murder by indifference.

Reflecting and Recording

Spend two or three minutes examining this statement: The opposite of love is not hate but apathy.

■ ■ ■

Continue your reflection by pondering the words of Elie Wiesel's character, Michael: "Betray, and you are a man; torture your neighbor; you're still a man. Evil is human, weakness is human; indifference is not."

■ ■ ■

What is the most painful experience of indifference you have known? Describe that experience here. Name persons. Tell what they did. How did you feel? How did you respond?

Is there anything "unfinished" about the experience you have described? Are you still feeling pain? Are you harboring resentment? Do you need to forgive? Stay with these questions for a few minutes.

■ ■ ■

What is the most painful experience you have inflicted upon another by your indifference, your failure to care? Describe that experience. Name the person. What did you do or fail to do? How do you think he or she felt? How did he or she respond? How did you feel?

Is there anything unfinished about the experience you have described? Have you asked the person to forgive you? Have you confessed your sin to the Lord? Is there any further action you need to take?

■ ■ ■

During the Day

Do some of the things you decided you need to do in your above reflections. If you can't do them all today, make a plan for doing them.

DAY 7

Faintheartedness and Slackness in Spiritual Growth

We want Christ, but only moderately: we love Jesus, but only moderately; we will follow Jesus, but only so far. To claim to be a Christian without wanting Christ more than anything else is a contradiction.

—Donald J. Shelby, from his sermon, "Wanting It Enough"

How passionate is our desire to follow Jesus? to be like him? to abide in him so that we are renewed in strength daily and reflect his likeness to the world? Jesus' word to us is clear:

I am the true vine, and my Father is the vinegrower. He removes every branch in me that bears no fruit. Every branch that bears fruit he prunes to make it bear more fruit. You have already been cleansed by the word that I have spoken to you. Abide in me as I abide in you. Just as the branch cannot bear fruit by itself unless it abides in the vine, neither can you unless you abide in me. I am the vine, you are the branches. Those who abide in me and I in them bear much fruit, because apart from me you can do nothing.

—John 15:1-5

According to Henry Fairlie, "Sloth has been described in theology as 'hatred of all spiritual things which entail effort,' and 'faintheartedness in matters of difficulty,' in striving for perfection." (Fairlie, p. 123) The parson in Chaucer's *Canterbury Tales* says sloth will "endure no hardship nor any penance."

There are three distinct forms of sloth. One, mental sloth. Though not always obvious, it is very common. Too lazy to think, to read, to enter into challenging dialogue, we take our opinions from favorite newspaper columnists, television newscasters, talk-show hosts, or television preachers. We end up not with solid opinion which we are willing to "go to the mat for," but with a collection of prejudices. Says Brian Whitlow in *Hurdles to Heaven*, "Prejudice is a great labor-saving device: It enables [us] to advance opinions without taking the trouble to get the facts."

Moral sloth is another form of this sin. We complain and complain about social and moral evil—racism, welfare, abortion, prison reform, violence in our schools, teenage drug abuse—but we don't do anything. We are too lazy to join an advocacy group or participate in a political party or share in the ministry of our church, which seeks redemption and reconciliation. Then there is the third form, more damning than the rest—spiritual sloth. *Why bother,* we ask ourselves, *when the spiritual quest becomes demanding and nothing we do seems to make much difference?*

When we neglect prayer, worship, Bible study, and other spiritual disciplines, we pay the price of shriveled and listless souls, and encounter the third form of sloth—spiritual sloth. Spiritual disciplines keep the wells of refreshment and renewal full of fresh water. Spiritual laziness dries them up and leaves no possibility but parched and dry souls.

The book of Psalms is full of the desolation in store for those slothful in spiritual things. Here are words from Psalm 107:

> Some wandered in desert wastes, finding no way to an inhabited town; hungry and thirsty, their soul fainted within them. . . .
>
> Some sat in darkness and in gloom, prisoners in misery and in irons, for they had rebelled against the words of God, and spurned the counsel of the Most High. Their hearts were bowed down with hard labor; they fell down, with no one to help. . . .
>
> They mounted up to heaven, they went down to the depths; their courage melted away in their calamity.
>
> —Psalm 107:4-5, 10-12, 26-27

Diligence, discipline, fortitude, perseverance—only these can protect us from the spiritual death sloth brings. A struggle for holiness and a hatred for sin must characterize our journey. The growing Christian is marked by a sense of sorrow for the part sin has in him. The holier we become, the deeper is our sorrow for sin. This sorrow keeps us sensitive and is a resistant force to any expression of spiritual sloth.

Reflecting and Recording

The strongest defense against spiritual sloth is what is called a "rule of life." It is a commitment to certain disciplines for spiritual formation. John Wesley had two categories of means of grace from which we might design a "rule of life" for ourselves. The first category, called the *instituted means of grace,* consists of prayer, scripture, the Lord's Supper, fasting, and Christian conferencing (intentional sharing with other Christians).

The second category, called *prudential means of grace,* involves doing no harm, and doing good. Wesley called these two groups of disciplines "works of piety" and "works of grace."

Listed below are all these means of grace. From them, will you design at least a beginning "rule of life" to be your armor against the deadly sin of sloth? Put a check beside the discipline you will practice. Then in the second column list the timing of your practice (daily, weekly, monthly). In the third column describe how you will practice it—what you will do, how you will do it.

DISCIPLINE	TIMING	HOW I WILL PRACTICE
Prayer		
Scripture		
The Lord's Supper		
Fasting		
Christian Conferencing		
Do No Harm		
Do Good		

During the Day

Begin your practice of the "rule of life" you have just designed. Find someone whom you trust and appreciate who is not experiencing this workbook journey with you and tell him or her about what you are experiencing as you are dealing with the seven deadly sins.

Group Meeting for Week Five

The theme of this week has been sloth. As we discussed, it is easy for sloth to prevail in our efforts at spiritual discipline. It is also easy to take the lazy route in our group participation. The temptation is to "play it safe" and not risk being honest and vulnerable.

Energy is another issue. Listening and speaking demands physical as well as emotional energy. So the temptation is to hold back, to be only half-present, not to invest the attention and focus essential for full participation.

We urge you to withstand these temptations. These sharing sessions are very important. Don't underestimate the value of each person's contribution. Stay sensitive to the possibility of slinking into laziness.

Sharing Together

1.   Begin your time together by the leader offering an opening prayer or calling on someone else (consulted ahead of time) to do so. Then sing a chorus or a couple of verses of a hymn everyone knows.
2.   Ask each person to share the most challenging and meaningful insight or experience gained from this week.
3.   Are there persons in the group who have problems "doing nothing"? Invite them to share their struggle. In light of their personality type, how do they relate to the general issue of laziness?
4.   Spend eight to twelve minutes discussing this claim: It is laziness that prevents us from loving.
     A.   Explore the issue in the context of love being an act of the will and laziness poisoning the will.
     B.   Invite two or three persons to share their own experiences, or an experience about which they know, where laziness prevented loving.
5.   Invite a person or two to share an experience where a relationship was seriously damaged or destroyed because of a person's unwillingness to love as an act of the will (Day 3).
6.   Spend five to ten minutes discussing the claim that sloth is connected with affluence. Do you believe that where there is abundance people tend not simply to satisfy their needs but to satiate themselves?
7.   Turn to page 110 in your workbook where questions about your community are asked. Read each of these questions and respond as a group.
8.   Invite two or three persons to share the most painful experiences of indifference they have known (Day 6).

9.   Spend eight to ten minutes discussing the following statements:
   * Apathy, not hate, is the opposite of love.
   * "Betray, and you are a man; torture your neighbor; you're still a man. Evil is human, weakness is human; indifference is not."
10.   Spend the balance of your sharing time discussing moral and spiritual sloth and where you see these operative in you, in your community, and in the nation.

Praying Together

Spontaneous conversational prayer is a creative and guiding source in our corporate life. Close your time together by inviting as many as will to offer brief prayers growing out of your sharing tonight. Before you begin this, ask if anyone in the group has specific prayer requests, especially areas where guidance is being sought.

When as many as wish to have prayed, close by inviting all to pray together the Lord's Prayer.

Week Six

Avarice
Excessive, Unbridled
Desire

DAY 1

Abundance of Possessions/Abundant Life

I came that they may have life, and have it abundantly" (John 10:10). Jesus said that. We could spend a long time pondering what the abundant life means. One of the convictions of this workbook adventure is that any and all of the seven deadly sins rob us of the abundant life Jesus offers.

Jesus made it especially clear as it relates to the sin at which we look this week: avarice. "Be on your guard against all kinds of greed; for one's life does not consist in the abundance of possessions" (Luke 12:15). Having an abundance of possessions is not the same as having "abundant life." As suggested by this particular warning of Jesus, avarice may be seen as covetousness; it may also be seen as greed. These are not the same—and there are shades of meaning in avarice that neither greed nor covetousness captures. These varying shades of meaning teach us needed lessons related to abundant life. We will consider these in the days ahead. For now, our emphasis is on the limitations of an abundance of things.

Many political analysts believe that the genius of Ronald Reagan in his bid for the United States presidency in 1980 was his asking the simple question: "Are you better off today than you were four years ago?" He kept pounding that question, making the state of our national economy the pivotal issue but also appealing to the economic fears of people. Even though he was not talking about greed or covetousness, the question itself is helpful as we consider the snare into which we often fall: thinking that abundance of possessions can provide abundant life. It's the misleading and ultimately destructive "arithmetic of affluence." Jesus told a parable about it:

And he said to them, "Take care! Be on your guard against all kinds of greed; for one's life does not consist in the abundance of possessions." Then he told them a parable: "The land of a rich man produced abundantly. And he thought to himself, 'What should I do, for I have no place to store my crops?' Then he said, 'I will do this: I will pull down my barns and build larger ones, and there I will store all my grain and my goods. And I will say to my soul, 'Soul, you have ample goods laid up for many years; relax, eat, drink, be merry.' But God said to him, 'You fool! This very night your life is being demanded of you. And the things you have prepared, whose will they be?' So it is with those who store up treasures for themselves but are not rich toward God."

—Luke 12:15-21

Had the farmer been right—if the materialist is really in fact the realist in our midst—then our friend Mel Wheatley is right. In "Bless Your Soul," one of his sermons, Mel made this statement: "The arithmetic of affluence should go something like this: If one barn makes a man ten percent happy, then ten barns—or their equivalent—should make the same man one hundred percent happy." But it doesn't work that way, does it? Our generation has ten times more things than any preceding generation. We doubt if we are ten times happier. With the possibility of some exceptions, you who are reading this have possessions beyond the most extravagant dreams of your parents. But ask yourself these questions: Am I better adjusted to life? Am I more secure? Do I handle trials and tribulations any better? Are temptations less seductive?

Your answers to these questions will answer the big question: Does abundance of possessions equal the abundant life?

Reflecting and Recording

Write a one- or two-sentence definition of the following words:

Greed

Covetousness

Enough

Spend a few minutes looking at your own life. Do you ever ask yourself, *How much is enough?* Is there anything about your life that would hint at the fact that you believe abundance of possessions will give you the happiness and meaning you are looking for?

■ ■ ■

During the Day

Look around you as you move through the day. Do you see places where persons are tearing down their barns to build bigger barns?

DAY 2

Avarice, Greed, Covetousness—
Some Helpful Distinctions

Yesterday we mentioned the fact that there are shades of meaning in avarice that neither covetousness nor greed captures. One helpful distinction is this: Covetousness is a desire for things we do not have; avarice is a hoarding of things we have but don't need. This distinction may be made between covetousness and greed: Greed is an inordinate desire for more and more; covetousness is greed flavored by jealousy, making it the desire for something someone else has.

Whatever the shade of meaning, selfishness is the common denominator. In his classic novel, *The Brothers Karamazov*, Fyodor Dostoyevsky tells the parable of the onion. It is a convicting description of the destructiveness of selfishness:

> Once upon a time, there was a peasant woman and a very wicked woman she was. And she died and did not leave a single good deed behind. The devils caught her and plunged her into the lake of fire. So her guardian angel stood and wondered what good deed of hers he could remember to tell to God; "she once pulled up an onion in her garden," said he, "and gave it to a beggar woman." And God answered, "You take that onion then, hold it out to her in the lake, and let her take hold and be pulled out. And if you can pull her out of the lake, let her come to Paradise, but if the onion breaks, then the woman must stay where she is." The angel ran to the woman and held out the onion to her; "Come," said he, "catch hold and I'll pull you out." And he began cautiously pulling her out. He had just pulled her right out, when the other sinners in the lake, seeing how she was being drawn out, began catching hold of her so as to be pulled out with her. But she began kicking them. "I'm to be pulled out, not you. It's my onion, not yours." As soon as she said that, the onion broke. And the woman fell back into the lake and she is burning there to this day. So the angel wept and went away.
>
> —Dostoyevsky, pp. 423–424

Avarice is selfishness, expressed in hoarding what we don't need, refusing to share. Covetousness is selfishness expressed in desiring what other people have that we don't, or specifically desiring something which belongs to someone else. Greed is selfishness expressed in always wanting more.

Someone has defined *enough* as "a little more than what you have." In light of these definitions go back and reconsider the definitions of greed, covetousness, and enough which you recorded yesterday.

Spend a bit of time reflecting on these shades of meaning.

■ ■ ■

In his second letter, Peter talks about the punishment that is going to come to the ungodly. Making the dramatic case for the fact that sinners will not escape judgment, he begins, "If God did not spare the angels when they sinned, but cast them into hell and committed them to chains of deepest darkness to be kept until the judgment . . ." (2 Pet. 2:4).

He goes on, scanning history, and recording the signal times of God's judgment: the flood, Sodom and Gomorrah. Then he says there are others who will reap the same condemnation:

> These people, however, are like irrational animals, mere creatures of instinct, born to be caught and killed. They slander what they do not understand, and when those creatures are destroyed, they also will be destroyed, suffering the penalty for doing wrong. They count it a pleasure to revel in the daytime. They are blots and blemishes, reveling in their dissipation while they feast with you. They have eyes full of adultery, insatiable for sin. They entice unsteady souls. They have hearts trained in greed. Accursed children!
>
> —2 Peter 2:12-14

It's a scathing condemnation, and we might pass it off as too extreme to apply to us except for that one designation—"hearts trained in greed." We might even evade relating that designation to ourselves by some mental sidestepping. But if we linger with it for a while, stay open, and allow scripture to speak to us, then we have to reckon with its relevance to us. The work may not be complete. Our heart may not yet be completely "trained in greed," but is the training going on?

Reflecting and Recording

Let's examine ourselves to see to what degree we are being trained in greed, covetousness, or avarice.

Greed: Have there been occasions in the past three months when you have desired more and more money or things than you really needed? Describe that experience in two or three sentences.

Covetousness: Describe in two or three sentences the last time you remember coveting— desiring a specific thing that belonged to someone else, or desiring something not because you needed it but wanting it because someone else had it.

Avarice: Are you hoarding things you don't need? If the word *hoarding* is too strong, think of the clothes in your closet that you have not worn in a long time, and probably will never wear again. Yet you hold on to them. For what purpose? Let this and/or some other common fact of most middle-class life, such as cans of food on your pantry shelves that have been there for weeks, stimulate three or four minutes of self-examination about avarice.

■ ■ ■

Close your time by praying that Christ will deliver you from that which is training your heart in greed, covetousness, or avarice.

During the Day

Did you look yesterday for demonstrations of "tearing down barns to build bigger barns"? Continue your focus today—paying attention to expressions of greed, covetousness, and avarice. Pay special attention to your own reactions and responses, not only to things but to persons. Guard against anything that even hints at greed or covetousness or avarice on your part.

DAY 3

Rich toward God

Go back and read Luke 12:15-21 printed on Day 1.

■ ■ ■

Jesus' parable closes with a powerful word: "So it is with those who store up treasures for themselves but are not rich toward God" (Luke 12:21).

The truth is this: What we can grasp (possessions) will never make us rich toward God, and what can make us rich toward God cannot be grasped. Put another way, again in the words of Mel Wheatley, "The things we can grasp will not fully satisfy us when they are reached. And what is more, that which does satisfy us can be reached for, but never fully grasped."

The more we have, the more we want. We keep grasping, spending ourselves—our time and energy and resources—for money, for toys, for gadgets, for things. We've seen it on bumper stickers: "He who dies with the most toys wins." Jesus says no to that. " 'You fool! This very night your life is being demanded of you. And the things you have prepared, whose will they be?' So it is with those who store up treasures for themselves but are not rich toward God" (Luke 12:20-21).

There are basically two views or images of the world: the secular and the religious. The secular image is materialistic and centers on the self. Persons with this perspective say, "I am the only reality. There is nothing out there. The world is indifferent to me." Though admittedly an oversimplification, it captures perceived reality.

The religious image, particularly the Christian vision, is that the world is not indifferent to us. Something is out there. No—*Someone* is out there. We are not accidents of biology but creatures of a loving God whose care and concern have been revealed to us in Jesus.

Avarice, greed, and covetousness are expressions of our distorted view of the world: The world is indifferent, there is nothing more than this. We have only ourselves and each other. Let's eat, drink, and be merry!

Don Blanding gave up his "eat, drink, and be merry" philosophy and began to reach for that which can satisfy, but can never be fully grasped. In *Joy Is an Inside Job* he explains:

> I knew that there was Something . . . Some Way . . . Some Answer. I'd better not wait *too* long to find out about it. . . . I searched the religions, faiths and cults of the world. I read Yogi and ate Yogurt. I read psychology, psychiatry, psychoanalysis, Dianetics, diarhettics, mental science, will-power, occultism and cultism. I gulped Physics, metaphysics and plain physics. I ended up with a fine case of Muddlephysics. There was a Shining Thread running through All of this . . . it was the deep realization that in the Power of the Presence of God-Consciousness, not as a remote and distant thing to be pled for, but an immediate and ever-present power, awaiting only recognition and acceptance, lies . . . the Peace of Heart which is beyond any other treasure, tangible or intangible, in the world.
>
> —Blanding, p. 24, 38

Don discovered that he was more than a body, more than senses to be satisfied, more than physical hungers to be fed. He had become rich toward God.

Reflecting and Recording

Has there been a time in your life when you thought money or things could make you happy? Be honest and make enough notes here to get in touch with that experience. What brought that conviction on? How long did it last? What happened to change your perspective?

In the above instruction for reflection, it was assumed that if you had ever thought money or things could make you happy, that is not your perspective now. Think about it. Is the assumption wrong? Are you ordering your life as though money and things could bring happiness?

■ ■ ■

During the Day

Yesterday, in your Reflecting and Recording time, you were asked to spend three or four minutes in self-examination about avarice—whether you were hoarding things you didn't need. If you concluded that you were, could you give away some of what you are hoarding today? If not today, make plans as to when you will.

DAY 4

How Much Is Enough?

James paints a frightening picture of our coveting and craving.

> Those conflicts and disputes among you, where do they come from? Do they not come from your cravings that are at war within you? You want something and do not have it; so you commit murder. And you covet something and cannot obtain it; so you engage in disputes and conflicts. You do not have, because you do not ask.
>
> —James 4:1-2

Is the case that extreme? Yes. The evidence appears on television news and the newspaper every day. A teenager is murdered for a pair of tennis shoes. A man rapes and beats a woman in broad daylight in New York City's Central Park. A tobacco industry scientist testifies that his company knew that nicotine acts like a drug on the brain and that the company carefully controlled the nicotine levels in cigarettes in order for users to become addicted. A mother sells her thirteen-year-old daughter into sexual bondage.

Dramatic? Bizarre? Yes, but they confirm what James says about the destructiveness of our coveting and craving. We don't have to think in the extreme. Our cravings play havoc in our lives. So we need to keep asking, "How much is enough?"

It helps us to think that the goods of the world are of three kinds: those that are necessary, those that are useful, and those that are "extra"—luxuries. What are the bare necessities? Food, clothing, shelter. The food doesn't have to be gourmet; name-brand clothing at exorbitant prices is not essential. And what "bare" need is met by the address of our shelter on "Snob Hill"?

Apart from the bare essentials of food, clothing, and shelter, there are useful things . . . things that make us more comfortable, tools that make our work easier and more efficient, books and art that enhance our growth and appreciation for life, enough entertainment and pleasure that provide healthy diversion from labor and routine. Like the necessities, though, are these useful things fewer in number, and could they not be far less expensive than runaway consumerism has made them?

Then there are luxuries. And for how many of us have luxuries become necessities? The question "How much is enough?" reveals the deadly sin of greed, gluttony, and lust. We desire and never have enough.

There is nothing wrong with having money and/or having the things that money can buy. The question is, Does money have us? Do we possess what we own or do our possessions own us?

Paul did not say that money is the root of all evil; he said the *love* of money is evil's root. "The love of money is a root of all kinds of evil, and in their eagerness to be rich some have wandered away from the faith and pierced themselves with many pains" (1 Tim. 6:10).

Riches are not evil, but they are dangerous. Note what Paul said, "In their eagerness to be rich some have wandered away from the faith and pierced themselves with many pains." Having too much can lead us to pride and more covetousness. More dangerous than anything, it can divert us from reliance on God. We'll talk more about this on Day 6.

Reflecting and Recording

Spend some time thinking on these questions:

Do I possess what I own, or does what I own possess me?

Look at the past fifteen years of your life. Have any of the things you considered luxuries in the past become necessities?

Is there a person you know whose possessions have diverted him or her from dependence on God?

Has anything near that—diversion from dependence on God—happened to you? Do you feel the threat of it?

■ ■ ■

During the Day

As you move through the day, make mental notes of the world's goods that come to you. In what category do they fall: necessities, useful items, luxuries?

DAY 5

Coldhearted

In *What Is Sin? What Is Virtue?* Robert J. McCracken paints an ugly picture of avarice.

Avarice! Note its last three letters—ice. In etymological origin, the word miser denotes a person who is miserable. It would never occur to an artist to portray an avaricious person with a spring in his step or a smile on his face. . . . Why is avarice a deadly sin? It isn't enough to say that it is ugly and harmful and leads to unhappiness. Let it begin to dominate a man and it will finally destroy him—ice in the heart, ulcers in the stomach, penury in the soul.

—McCracken, pp. 34–35

Avarice is an ugly sin. It makes people ugly. Dorothy L. Sayers groups the seven deadly sins into two categories: the three warmhearted and disrespectable sins—lust, gluttony, and anger; and the four coldhearted and respectable sins—pride, sloth, envy, and avarice. Avarice is coldhearted. Avarice is self-love in one of its most perverted forms. It is protecting ourselves and hoarding what we have. We can hold a penny so close to our eye that it blocks out the sun. Avarice does that. It blocks out the light of love and concern for others. We have never known a happy miser. Stingy folks hardly ever smile. They are closed in on themselves because in their avarice they close others out.

Not so with generous people. They are happy. Giving gives them joy. I remember Mary, one of the few people in our middle- to upper-middle-class community, living far below the defined poverty level. Her total income was the $107 Social Security check she received monthly. Of that she paid $55 for rent, leaving $52 for food, clothing, and bare necessities. Her apartment was always cold and dimly lighted. In order to provide some additional income, Mary rendered typing services for me. Hardly ever would she receive an outright gift of money. Only once—when she had little food and no money for two weeks—did I see her sorely depressed. Despite Mary's destitution, her attention was always fixed on seeking ways to give herself to others. She taught Mexican-Americans to read and speak English in a volunteer literacy program.

I remember my last visit with this woman before she moved from our city. She showed me a coat and two dresses she had purchased at Goodwill Industries with money she could ill afford to spend. They were gifts for the daughters of one of her Mexican-American students. I lost contact with my friend and knew nothing of her whereabouts for over a year. Then came a marvelous letter in which she told me that she had entered junior college. Imagine that: nearly seventy, in very poor health, but still alive! Here are some excerpts from that letter:

I'm very happy here, among all the interesting young people. (I feel much more at home with them than with people of my own age . . .) I was afraid of the youth—that they would make fun of me and my clothes, and being old, but they are far more broad-minded than older people. I do some tutoring in Spanish, not for money, for these are poor people, and it wouldn't be right.

Mary demonstrates the truth that life is the chance God gives us to learn how to love and give ourselves away. Pity—too many never learn the lesson.

In *Giving USA* (an annual philanthropy report) statistics show that households earning less than $5,000 per year gave 5.9 percent of their income while households earning $100,000 to $150,000 gave 4.1 percent. Those earning $500,000 to $1,000,000 per year gave only 3.7 percent of their income.

Do these statistics point to *avarice?* Do they say something about coldheartedness? Do they underscore these words of Jesus: "Truly I tell you, it will be hard for a rich person to enter the kingdom of heaven. Again I tell you, it is easier for a camel to go through the eye of a needle than for someone who is rich to enter the kingdom of God"? (Matt. 19:23-24).

Do you remember the story that Jesus told before pronouncing this hard truth—the story of a young rich man?

> Then someone came to [Jesus] and said, "Teacher, what good deed must I do to have eternal life?" And he said to him, "Why do you ask me about what is good? There is only one who is good. If you wish to enter into life, keep the commandments." He said to him, "Which ones?" And Jesus said, "You shall not murder; You shall not commit adultery; You shall not steal; You shall not bear false witness; Honor your father and mother; also, You shall love your neighbor as yourself." The young man said to him, "I have kept all these; what do I still lack?" Jesus said to him, "If you wish to be perfect, go, sell your possessions, and give the money to the poor, and you will have treasure in heaven; then come, follow me." When the young man heard this word, he went away grieving, for he had many possessions.
>
> —Matthew 19:16-22

Why did Jesus make that demand of the young man? He knew that he could not love and serve God completely until he put his money in a different position of priority in his life. What we really love determines who we are. When we consider the devastating numbers of persons—statistics show that these are in the thousands and some case millions—who die of starvation each day, go to sleep hungry each night, and babies who go blind every year due to lack of vitamin A in their diets, we see the grim effects of greed.

Though not the complete cause, the avarice and greed of the American people are factors contributing to these tragedies. There is only one way to overcome our coldheartedness: to give ourselves to Jesus so completely that we will begin to give ourselves and our resources to others.

Reflecting and Recording

On Day 3 we considered being "rich toward God." Name the first three persons that come to your mind whom you would consider "rich toward God."

(1)

(2)

(3)

Think about each of these persons now. Are they generous with their time and money? Do they share their homes? Do they welcome strangers? Are they worried about money or other material things? Are they stingy? By each name make some notes about the above-named persons with these questions in mind.

■ ■ ■

Avarice is coldhearted—protecting itself and hoarding what it has. Spend the balance of your time honestly looking at your life as it relates to this sin. To what degree is avarice present in the way you make decisions and relate to others?

■ ■ ■

During the Day

Look for ways to give yourself—your time, energy, money—in little ways today that may make a big difference.

DAY 6

Greed Diverts Our Reliance on God

Then [Jesus] looked up at his disciples and said: "Blessed are you who are poor, for yours is the kingdom of God. Blessed are you who are hungry now, for you will be filled. Blessed are you who weep now, for you will laugh. Blessed are you when people hate you, and when they exclude you, revile you, and defame you on account of the Son of Man. Rejoice in that day and leap for joy, for surely your reward is great in heaven; for that is what their ancestors did to the prophets. But woe to you who are rich, for you have received your consolation. Woe to you who are full now, for you will be hungry.

Woe to you who are laughing now, for you will mourn and weep. Woe to you when all speak well of you, for that is what their ancestors did to the false prophets."

—Luke 6:20-26

This is Luke's presentation of what we call the Beatitudes. In Matthew's Gospel, the Beatitudes come at the beginning of Jesus' Sermon on the Mount. There they are succinct pronouncements designating the "blessed"—those who have abundant and eternal life, beginning with "Blessed are the poor in spirit, for theirs is the kingdom of heaven" (Matt. 5:3).

Luke records most of the content of the Beatitudes, but in different form, and with a stronger emphasis on the role that "this world's goods" play in our relation to God and whether we will receive the reward of heaven. He doesn't say, as Matthew puts it, "poor in spirit," but simply, "Blessed are you who are poor." He doesn't say "hunger and thirst for righteousness," but those "who are hungry now."

Matthew does record that Jesus talked about the use of money and giving gifts in his Sermon on the Mount, but Matthew does not connect it directly with the Beatitudes. Luke, whose Gospel is often referred to as "the Gospel to the poor," doesn't want us to miss the inevitable connection between what we have and how we use it and our relationship to God: "But woe to you who are rich, for you have received your consolation. Woe to you who are full now, for you will be hungry" (Luke 6:24-25).

We come back to the truth we introduced on Day 4: More dangerous than anything else, having too much can divert us from reliance on God. That's what Jesus was saying in Luke's record of his teaching. Someone has put it starkly: You will never know that Jesus is all you need, until Jesus is all you've got.

The greedy accumulation of things is one of the most glaring ways we evade our dependence on God. Avarice, the hoarding of money and things, is a sure sign that we do not trust God. Covetousness, inordinately desiring what others have, reveals a distorted notion that possessions, not our relationship with God, are what give us meaning.

Reflecting and Recording

Has there ever been a time in your life when "Jesus was all you had"? Describe that experience here.

Is there anything in your life that is a sure sign that you do not trust God completely? Name and describe that sign.

Spend the balance of your time reflecting on whether what you have—your possessions, earnings, security, job—is diverting you from a total reliance on God.

■ ■ ■

During the Day

You have probably seen it on a bumper sticker, as a beautiful placard, on business cards, printed boldly on tee-shirts, even on coffee mugs: *Practice Random Kindness and Senseless Acts of Beauty.* How the slogan came about and spread is worth consideration. I've heard that it emerged mysteriously, appeared out of nowhere, as it were, in the San Francisco area.

A woman visiting a friend saw a card on the refrigerator that said, "Practice random kindness and senseless acts of beauty."

The next day she tried it. She was going across the Bay Bridge to San Francisco. She gave the man in the tollbooth seven commuter tickets and said, "This is for me and for the next six people in line behind me." One after another, the cars came up to the tollbooth with hands out the window holding dollar bills to pay the toll collector. He just waved the drivers on across the bridge, saying, "It's taken care of—have a nice day."

Well, we imagine those people did have a nice day—we even imagine that the people with whom they worked had a nice day as well.

Then that same sign the woman had seen on a refrigerator door appeared as graffiti on a wall: "Practice random kindness and senseless acts of beauty." Another woman saw that. She wrote it down and gave it to her husband, who is a seventh-grade teacher. He put it on the blackboard in the classroom. One of his students copied it down and showed it to her mother, who is a newspaper columnist. She wrote about it in the newspaper, asking, "Where did this come from?" Two days later she heard from Ann Herbert from Marin County, California. She confessed. She had thought of it while sitting in a Sausalito restaurant and had written it down on a paper placemat. The man next to her saw it, copied it down, and that's how it got started. Now it's spreading.

We invite you to continue spreading it. This day, pay attention to every encounter with people, grasp every opportunity to "practice random kindness and senseless acts of beauty." It's a great antidote for greed and sloth.

DAY 7

Greed "Shutteth up . . . Bowels of Compassion"

I used to work downtown in the Morgan Keegan building. Late one afternoon, about 6 P.M., I took a break and walked over to the little supermarket across the street that has a counter at the back where they make sandwiches. I went to get a sandwich and drink for supper.

When I approached the front door, I noticed a man—a street person—peering intently into the store. I had to ask him to step aside so I could get in the door. Seeing him there reminded me at that time of my neighbor's dog who would follow us to the Minit-Mart in Jackson and sit squarely in front of the door, peering in, until we came out. I later realized what was the object of his interest.

After I had picked up a sandwich and a Coke, I stood in line to check out. A "street person" was in line behind me. As I was standing there, this man behind me mumbled something like, "So little for so many." I asked him what he meant and he told me he was buying what he could to feed himself and his friends, and all he could buy was some hamburger meat and a loaf of white bread. They couldn't build a fire for the hamburger so they were going to eat raw hamburger sandwiches.

Something inside me said, "Do something," so I took the man to the back of the store to get some sandwiches, milk, and chips. The store management was concerned and wanted the man to leave. I said no, the man wasn't bothering me; I just wanted to buy him some food.

Anyway, while we were waiting for the sandwiches, I asked the man if he had any family and where he was from. He had a family but through various circumstances he had failed them and lost his job and become a street person—a "bum," as he put it. He said he had a son and daughter he had not seen in many years, but they didn't love him anymore and were embarrassed by his lifestyle.

I showed him pictures of my children. I told him I bet that his children would still love him and would help him, welcome him back, if he would just call. He started crying.

To make this story short, after I paid for the food, which he promptly distributed to the man at the door and three or four others I had not seen, I convinced him to call his daughter. There are pay phones on the mall. I gave him a dollar in quarters and he called his daughter. After a few minutes on the phone, he came back with tears in his eyes. He told me his daughter, who lived in Jackson, Tennessee, was coming to pick him up. He was going home!

What a story! Our friend Nash Neyland had shared it in a letter in which he was telling what was going on in his life and seeking counsel on some big decisions. What did such a moving story have to do with his decisions? He went on:

Great story, huh! Only it never happened. Yes, I did go to the grocery store for a sandwich. I did see a street person at the front door, peering in. Yes, there was a street person standing in line behind me and yes, he did say something like "so little for so many." And yes, something inside of me said, "Do something." But instead of doing something, I did nothing. I didn't even talk to him.

Our friend couldn't get over what he called his "opportunity lost," and was seeking guidance about how he was going to order his life, given more expansive "opportunities" to serve.

Neither avarice nor greed nor covetousness was operating in our friend's life in any sort of self-conscious awareness. He is a generous person who intentionally seeks to be a faithful disciple. The story, however, dramatically pictures the all-too-common failure of even the most faithful Christians among us in using the gifts with which we have been blessed.

Our friend is haunted by his "opportunity lost," as well he should be, for one of the telling and judging words of scripture speaks to the issue. "How does God's love abide in anyone who has the world's goods and sees a brother or sister in need and yet refuses help?" (1 John 3:17).

The word is even more hard hitting in its larger context:

This is the message you have heard from the beginning, that we should love one another. We must not be like Cain who was from the evil one and murdered his brother. And why did he murder him? Because his own deeds were evil and his brother's righteous. Do not be astonished, brothers and sisters, that the world hates you. We know that we have passed from death to life because we love one another. Whoever does not love abides in death. All who hate a brother or sister are murderers, and you know that murderers do not have eternal life abiding in them. We know love by this, that he laid down his life for us—and we ought to lay down our lives for one another. How does God's love abide in anyone who has the world's goods and sees a brother or sister in need and yet refuses help?

—1 John 3:11-17

John does not want us to miss the point. Refusing to use our world's goods to meet the needs of another is the same sin as Cain murdering his brother, and allowing hatred to grow for any sister or brother. John sets this in contrast to the love demonstrated in the death of Christ: "He [Christ] laid down his life for us—and we ought to lay down our lives for one another."

The classic King James translation of verse 17 paints the picture more graphically: "But whoso hath this world's good, and seeth his brother have need, and shutteth up his bowels of compassion from him, how dwelleth the love of God in him?" (1 John 3:17). The language, though maybe at first not understood, gets our attention. "Bowels of compassion"—both Testaments often place the seat of our deepest feelings in our stomachs—less elegantly stated, in our "gut." So we talk about "gut reaction." "Bowels of mercy" is a phrase in scripture to express our deepest feelings.

John talks about closing down, shutting off our "bowels of compassion"—a sure sign that the love of God is not operative in us.

Avarice, greed, and covetousness do that—they "shut up our bowels of compassion."

Reflecting and Recording

Look back over the last three or four months of your life. List four occasions when you had the opportunity to show compassion, to share yourself and your resources, but did not. In a few words, identify those experiences.

(1)

(2)

(3)

(4)

Now go back and describe the experiences more fully. Was it money, or food, or time, or energy you didn't share? Was it simply a matter of not being gracious, not paying attention? Were you too busy to get involved? Get in touch with those experiences by rethinking and reliving them. Make more notes.

■ ■ ■

Now think of an experience where you were confronted with need and responded to it. Make some notes about it.

Spend some time thinking about the last experience you described compared to the others. Which experience do you want as a way to characterize your life?

■ ■ ■

During the Day

Continue your random kindness and senseless acts of beauty.

Group Meeting for Week Six

Introduction

You are drawing to the close of this workbook venture. You have only two more planned group meetings. Your group may want to discuss the future. Would the group like to stay together for a longer time? Are there resources (books, tapes, periodicals) that the group would like to use corporately? If you are a part of the same church, is there some way you could share the experience you have had with others? Test the group to see if they would like to discuss future possibilities.

Sharing Together

1. Begin your sharing by spending only a few minutes—four to six—discussing the definition of enough as "a little more than what you have."
2. Invite each person to share his/her most difficult day with the workbook this week. Tell why that particular day was so difficult.
3. Turn to page 123 in your workbook where greed, covetousness, and avarice are described as shades of meaning for the same thing. After the leader reads about greed, allow one or two persons to share their personal responses. Continue the same with covetousness and avarice.
4. Turn to your Reflecting and Recording for Day 3 (page 126). Would two or three persons share their responses to the first questions?
5. Spend ten to fifteen minutes discussing the three kinds of the goods of the world: the necessary, the useful, the extra—how these are confused, how we change in our attitude toward them. Have what you considered luxuries in the past become essential?
6. Spend five to eight minutes discussing this claim: Riches are not evil but they are dangerous.
    A. What does the following statement have to do with the danger of riches? "The love of money, not money itself, is the root of evil."
    B. What does this statement have to do with the dangers of riches? "Do we possess what we own or does what we own possess us?"
7. On Day 5, you were asked to name three persons whom you considered "rich toward God." Would two persons describe in detail one of the persons they named?
8. Spend five to ten minutes discussing this assertion: *The greedy accumulation of things is one of the most glaring ways we evade our dependence on God* (Day 6).

9.   Spend the balance of your sharing time allowing persons to share experiences of extending compassion and failing to extend compassion. Reflect with one another on why we do or don't show compassion and the meaning these actions have in our lives.

Praying Together

We hope that you have been together enough to be honest and free in your praying as well as your discussion. Let your praying together be a "season of prayer," when any person in the group can offer a few sentences of prayer about any concern.

This can take on the structure of "conversational prayer." What one person prays will stimulate another to center his/her prayer. Spend as much time as necessary to allow all who wish to offer verbal prayer, then close with the group praying together the Lord's Prayer.

Week Seven

Lust
"The Craving for Salt of a Person Who Is Dying of Thirst"

DAY 1

The Secret Sin

A few years ago, before the fall of Communism, the Russian government experienced deep embarrassment at the hands of a nineteen-year-old German youth. He flew his single-engine Cessna Skyhawk 172 airplane hundreds of miles over Russian territory completely undetected, landing safely right in the middle of Red Square. While the world was amazed by this feat, the Communist government reacted by immediately arresting the young man and tossing him into prison. Apparently the young man was so wrapped up in the challenge of accomplishing this feat that he had scant regard for any possible consequences.

While we might not see it at first, this story is an illustration of lust: no thought of the consequences, no consideration of what might lie ahead, simply the thrill of a particular moment's challenge.

> It happened, late one afternoon, when David rose from his couch and was walking about on the roof of the king's house, that he saw from the roof a woman bathing; the woman was very beautiful. David sent someone to inquire about the woman. It was reported, "This is Bathsheba daughter of Eliam, the wife of Uriah the Hittite." So David sent messengers to get her, and she came to him, and he lay with her. (Now she was purifying herself after her period.) Then she returned to her house. The woman conceived; and she sent and told David, "I am pregnant."
>
> —2 Samuel 11:2-5

The best-known story of lust in the Bible is the story of David and Bathsheba. Poets and prose writers, preachers and movie-makers have had a field day since, retelling this story. They have used all the resources of language to describe David's lust, his burning passion, and to give the reader or viewer or listener a second-hand experience of exotic intrigue and satisfied lust. Like the young man flying into Russia and landing in Red Square, David didn't stop to think about the consequences. He wanted what he wanted, and being king, of course, he could get it.

Lust takes no thought of consequences; the thrill of a particular moment's challenge or the immediate satisfaction of sexual passion dominate relationship and action.

We have a difficult time talking about lust. We can talk rather easily about the other six deadly sins, but somehow, when we get to lust, all conversation stops. There are two reasons for our discomfort. The most obvious is that for the last several centuries or more, lust has been *the* deadly sin. Dorothy L. Sayers wrote an address on the seven deadly sins entitled "The Other Six Deadly Sins" because a young man came to her and said, "I did not know there were seven deadly sins: please tell me the names of the other six."

Historically, the church has been at its harshest and most unforgiving when dealing with the sins of lust, many times amplifying and intensifying already painful and humiliating situations. At the same time, the church has also been reticent to discuss the difficulties we human beings face in dealing with our sexual natures. We shouldn't be surprised, then, if people are afraid or embarrassed to discuss such matters.

The second reason we are uncomfortable dealing with the sin of lust is that in recent years we have come to see ourselves as liberated from the repressive sexual mores of the past. At first glance, it seems that liberation would lead to more open discussion. However, more often than not, it seems to have created a dilemma for us instead. If we are no longer confined to the "repressive" sexual mores of the past, then lust should no longer be a problem for us. Yet, it still rears its ugly head, wreaking havoc on our relationships, our family life, and our social fabric. Admitting that lust remains a problem leaves us open to charges of being "too uptight," of being "sexually inhibited," or even (and for some this is the worst) being "intolerant of the value of each person's unique sexual expression." Again, it shouldn't surprise us that people are reluctant to share their feelings on the topic of lust.

Reflecting and Recording

Spend some time thinking on these questions:

How has the church responded to the sin of lust? Have you known an instance or instances when the church dealt harshly—perhaps unforgivingly—with a person involved in sexual sin?

What role has the church played in your understanding of human sexuality?

Respond to this statement: We have come to see ourselves as liberated from the repressive sexual mores of the past.

■ ■ ■

How do you define lust? Write your definition here.

During the Day

In reading the newspaper, watching television, observing others, and paying attention to your own feelings and desires, identify occasions of lust.

DAY 2

Not Sex Alone

Yesterday we considered our reluctance to talk about lust. Despite that reluctance, despite a "new morality" that has glorified sex and supposedly freed us from the repressive mores of the past, lust is one of the most damaging of the seven deadly sins. It strikes at the core of our being, at that wild and seemingly uncontrollable center of ourselves, our sexuality. Frederick Buechner defined lust as "the craving for salt of a person who is dying of thirst." (*Wishful Thinking*, p. 54) In his letter to the Romans, Paul makes the case that uncontrolled lust is one of the most blatant and destructive signs of our refusal to honor God:

> Therefore God gave them up in the lusts of their hearts to impurity, to the degrading of their bodies among themselves, because they exchanged the truth about God for a lie and worshiped and served the creature rather than the Creator, who is blessed forever! Amen.
>
> —Romans 1:24-25

What makes dealing with the sin of lust so elusive is that it emanates from our deepest need and desire—love. Stephen Shoemaker put it eloquently when he wrote, "Persons trapped in sexual sin are trying so hard to love and be loved. Lust is especially poignant; it is the distortion of the highest good and purpose of life: love. It is so close to love and yet even in its closeness so painfully far away" (p. 102).

Because of both its power and its tenderness, it is imperative that we look honestly at the sin of lust and deal with its effect on our lives. How do we begin? What exactly are we talking about when we discuss the sin of lust? In the dictionary, lust has several definitions. Most of them involve sex, but they aren't limited to that domain. Here are a few: "intense sexual desire or appetite"; "uncontrolled or illicit sexual desire"; "a passionate or overmastering desire or craving"; "to have a strong or excessive craving." How does the way you defined lust in your Reflecting and Recording yesterday compare to these definitions?

■ ■ ■

Our purpose is to examine the sin of lust, so the common thread for us in these definitions, even if they aren't specifically about sex, are words like *uncontrolled, illicit, overmastering,* and *excessive.* We can be ambitious, but if we have a lust for power, then we have crossed into dangerous territory because our ambition has become excessive or uncontrolled. Just as ambition is not sinful in itself, neither is intense sexual longing, nor passion, nor desire. These were meant to be blessings to us, good gifts that enhance and enliven our existence. It is the context, however, that makes the difference. We find it telling that in definitions for lust, the dictionary usually includes the word *for* or *after*, as in *lust for* or *lust after*. Lust, then, always involves objects. At its most basic level, it is a preoccupation with objects of our desire. We lust *after* or *for* something or someone, not *with* something or someone.

Certainly, our main focus in discussing lust this week will be its sexual nature; however, lust is not limited solely to this realm. It is important for us to recognize how subtly intertwined lust is with many of the other deadly sins. Sometimes it is difficult to tell whether it is greed, pride, or a lust for power that is driving people as they claw and scratch their way up the ladder of "success." And the sly voice of envy, which leads us to believe that we should be able to have access to and experience everything that everyone else is able to have access to and experience, skillfully heightens our lust for all those things we have not yet encountered or experienced. Therefore, if we limit lust only to its sexual dimension, we leave ourselves vulnerable to its power to work destructively in other areas of our lives. So too, if we avoid the sexual arena altogether, we will surely suffer the pain lust inevitably leaves in its wake.

Reflecting and Recording

Take a few moments to focus on lust as a preoccupation with objects of our desire. Do you have a desire or goal or want about which you are preoccupied—job, money, image, social, family, sex? Name that desire or goal here and write a sentence or two about your quest for it.

Is your pursuit of this desire uncontrolled or excessive or overmastering? How does your attention or preoccupation lead you to treat others in your quest to obtain the object of your desire?

■ ■ ■

Spend two or three minutes reflecting on this understanding: Love treats people as persons; lust treats people as things.

■ ■ ■

Write a brief prayer expressing the struggle with lust in your life, asking the Lord to reveal unrecognized and unacknowledged lust and for the power to overcome.

During the Day

Stay aware of a preoccupation (lust *after* or *for* something or someone) that you might have, and offer prayer to overcome it.

DAY 3

From Repressed to Obsessed

Yesterday, we began our exploration of lust by focusing on preoccupation in a general way. We have many desires with which we may be preoccupied, and the inordinate amount of energy we expend in pursuit of those desires can be harmful to us and others. However, there is one area of desire which, if pursued lustfully, produces a uniquely deep and private pain and devastation: sex. This is where lust does its deadliest work. Human sexuality is a topic into which we must delve carefully, for there is no other aspect of our physical and emotional life that contains as much promise for intense joy or as much potential for profound suffering. There are two reasons such opposite possibilities can emerge from our sexuality—love and lust—and, as we mentioned yesterday, they are deceptively close to each other yet agonizingly far apart. Our task for the rest of the week will be to compare and contrast love and lust.

> Don't you know that your body is the temple of the Holy Spirit, who lives in you and who was given to you by God? You do not belong to yourselves but to God; he bought you for a price. So use your bodies for God's glory.
>
> —1 Corinthians 6:19-20, GNT

One of the issues that has led us to mistake lust for love is an unhealthy view of our bodies. Our bodies are not evil; rather they are wondrous miracles of a good and loving God—temples for the Holy Spirit. The repressive views of sexuality that have developed over the centuries stem from this unhealthy view of the body as evil. The Victorian idea that sex must be a somber and serious event, or that it was a painful part of a woman's wifely duty, certainly did not help people understand how to deal healthily with their sexual desire. Rather, it fueled their lust as they illicitly looked for partners who actually enjoyed sex, and then it fueled their guilt when they found them. God did not create sex to be a "necessary evil." On the contrary, it was given to us, as Anthony Campolo asserts, to be enjoyed "as a glorious foretaste of heaven."

A Victorian view of sexuality is not the predominant problem today, however. We have traded one unhealthy view of the body for another. Most of us no longer believe that our bodies are evil; rather, we exalt our bodies. Millions of dollars are spent each year on fitness equipment and exercise video tapes. Advertisements abound for creams and lotions and diets and drinks to help us look younger and firmer and thinner and sexier. The health of our bodies is a very important issue. If the body is, as we believe, the Temple of the Holy Spirit, then it should be treated with the utmost care, with appropriate attention given to its health. Yet even a casual glance at our society reveals that a balanced concern with our health is not what is motivating us; it is the image of our bodies that has captured our attention. The *temple* is what we worship rather than the Spirit of God who resides within it.

The shift in how we view our bodies has led to a shift in how we look at our sexuality. We have moved from being repressed to being obsessed. "People now seem to have sex on their minds," Malcolm Muggeridge once said, "which is a peculiar place to have it." He was right. We are obsessed with our bodies and with our sexuality. Therapists have said that men think about sex every three minutes and women think about it every six minutes. It colors our entire culture.

I don't think many people would argue that our societal obsession with sex has had tragic consequences: marriages destroyed, violence suffered, children exploited. However, it's often easy to let ourselves off the hook, particularly if we haven't actually committed any specific act. But Jesus made getting off the hook a lot harder when he said, "You have heard that it was said, 'You shall not commit adultery.' But I say to you that everyone who looks at a woman with lust has already committed adultery with her in his heart" (Matt. 5:27-28).

I don't believe Jesus was condemning everyone who has ever experienced the natural surge of sexual excitement; those feelings are a good, necessary, and important part of being human. To condemn them would be cruel. Yet, Jesus is demanding a great deal from us. The demand comes because the path of lust is so insidious. Sex never "just happens." It is always a step-by-step process, beginning with a look or a thought, and progressing, often so slowly as to go unnoticed, until it has wreaked its havoc. The demand also comes because, as we discussed yesterday, lust is an overmastering preoccupation. When we become preoccupied with an object that we desire, our energies are refocused in a new direction; other areas that might have previously commanded our attention no longer do so, leaving a void. It is no wonder that many persons instinctively sense when there is something "not right" about the way their partners are now relating to them, even when nothing has happened yet. So Jesus' words are not some harsh condemnation of our natural sexual appetites. They are a warning: Lust is a deadly preoccupation. Sometimes that preoccupation results in action, sometimes it does not; but always it disrupts healthy relationships and endangers promises of faithfulness.

Reflecting and Recording

Examining your own experience, what have your parents, trusted friends, and the church taught you to feel about your body and about sex?

■ ■ ■

Are you "glorifying" your body unduly—preoccupied with image, worshiping your body, rather than allowing your body to be the temple of the Holy Spirit?

■ ■ ■

Spend some time reflecting on this general truth: Sin is a good which has somehow become misdirected. Think about this specifically in terms of the sins we have considered in the past week. Make some notes about how the following sins are distortions or misdirections of good.

Pride

Envy

Anger

Sloth

Greed

To consider the possibility that lust is "a good which has somehow become misdirected," spend a few minutes pondering the assertion that God did not create sex to be a necessary evil but to be enjoyed as a "glorious foretaste of heaven."

■ ■ ■

Go back and read the prayer you wrote and prayed yesterday. Is there any awareness there of lust being the misdirection of good?

■ ■ ■

During the Day

Pay attention to the misdirection of good in your life—how a natural, good instinct, drive, or desire can be or is distorted.

DAY 4

Love and Lust

Contrary to many persons' hopes, the sexual revolution that eased the rigid nature of the Victorian era did not bring us the liberation that had been expected; it merely traded one type of bondage for another. Our sexual life may no longer be captive to guilt, but we do have a new oppressor: the pressure to say yes. There seems to be a cultural assumption that if we don't want to do something that we are biologically able to do, we must be repressing our natural instincts. This inhibition is almost always viewed as unhealthy. Thus we encounter surprise and sometimes hostility when we assert our desire not to participate. Date rape is a prime illustration of this.

We have not always used the term, but for the past twenty years at least, *date rape* has been understood in sociological studies of sexual practice. Sexual inhibitions have been publicly scorned. Sexual freedom and expression have been so glorified that young men are surprised when their dates say no. It is as though we have no right to say no. So the rising tide of date rape often is the result of peer pressure among teenagers and young adults to say yes to sexual intercourse; and sexual experimentation has never been greater than today.

The biblical view of sexuality avoids bondage to both the austere Victorian mores and to the pressure to say yes. As indicated yesterday, our bodies are not evil, with every sexual urge to be mastered and subdued. Nor are they divine and to be worshiped, with every desire taken as an opportunity to indulge in the pleasures of sex. Rather, a biblical theology of the body emphasizes that our bodies are temples for the Spirit of God. Building on a Christian understanding of the body, a biblical theology of sexuality asserts that the full meaning and joy of sex can only be experienced in the context of loving commitment. This is the reason the Bible teaches that sexual intercourse is to be reserved for the covenant of marriage. And this is the reason Jesus taught that marriage requires our deepest commitment:

> Some Pharisees came to him, and to test him they asked, "Is it lawful for a man to divorce his wife for any cause?" He answered, "Have you not read that the one who made them at the beginning 'made them male and female,' and said, 'For this reason a man shall leave his father and mother and be joined to his wife, and the two shall become one flesh'? So they are no longer two, but one flesh. Therefore what God has joined together, let no one separate."
>
> —Matthew 19:3-6

I can recall as a child all the suppressed giggles and significant looks exchanged between my friends and me any time an Old Testament passage was read that mentioned a man "knowing" his wife. We knew the code! We knew what they were really talking about! But that "code" is actually the first step in distinguishing between love and lust. In Hebrew, the word for "to know" and "to have sexual relations with" is the same: *yada'*. This is meaningful because it reminds us that for our sexuality to be healthy and most fully actualized, it must be a weaving together of longing and knowing. We will never be totally fulfilled in our sexual life until we have made the commitment to know deeply the one whom we desire. Conversely, we turn others into objects when we desire them sexually but have no interest in developing an intimate knowledge of them.

A major contrast between love and lust, then, is that love implies personal commitment. It requires effort and involvement. Lust is not interested in being involved or in the effort required for personal commitment. A discouraging aspect of our society today is that so many people participate in seemingly haphazard and aimless relationships that are over before they've even had a chance to begin. Love makes many demands. We are witnessing so much promiscuity because many people are no longer willing to meet those demands. Lust renders them uninterested in becoming involved or caring for another in anything other than the most superficial kinds of ways. The most flagrant expression of lust—and perhaps the most tragic—is when an individual has sex with someone about whom he or she does not care, and has no plan to ever care.

In a more subtle way we can also see the reluctance to commit in the reasoning of many young people who determine that they must live together first before marrying in order to make sure it will work. By leaving themselves a way out, they have sabotaged their relationship from the start and have fooled themselves about their true level of commitment. In our work as pastors, we have counseled with numerous persons, mostly women, who are devastated because their spouses took the easy way out of a "living-together" relationship because the commitment of marriage was not there as a "glue" to keep them together to work through the rough places. More often than not, persons feel used and disrespected, and often they suffer from shame and lack of self-respect—not only because a relationship has failed, but because they feel betrayed and dishonored as persons.

We like to think that love is the necessary ingredient for marriage, but it is the other way around. Marriage is a necessary ingredient for lasting love. Love, especially in the beginning, can be hard to distinguish from lust. Love can be strong and seem overpowering. Its flame is intense and bright. Love can also be ephemeral, disappearing as quickly as it came. But for love to develop and last, for its roots to grow deep and secure, it needs the commitment of marriage. Immediate response to lust may satisfy an immediate desire, but only love can satisfy the need of every human being.

Reflecting and Recording

Respond to this statement: Marriage is a necessary ingredient for lasting love.

■ ■ ■

For Married People Only

Take a long look at your marriage. How has your commitment to marriage been a primary source for your growth in love? Put another way, would you have grown in your love for your spouse had you not known the demands and constraints that the marriage commitment includes?

■ ■ ■

For Divorced People Only

What role did sexual lust and/or dissatisfaction with your sexual relationship with your former spouse play in leading to divorce? Has what you thought was missing sexually in your marriage been satisfied? If you had it to do over again, how would you relate and act differently?

■ ■ ■

During the Day

Pay attention to the billboards, the newspapers, TV, and magazine advertisements you see today. When "the body"—sex—is used, what is being said of the body? Offer this prayer: "Lord, help me to remember that my body is the temple of your Holy Spirit."

DAY 5

The Don Juan Syndrome

Lust is not interested in the requirements of commitment. It cares only for the challenge of the pursuit and conquest. Because that is its prime focus, it is a solitary and isolated endeavor, with self-gratification as its only goal. Lord Byron's *Don Juan* offers a relevant example. Continually searching for the elusive experience of complete satisfaction, the character of Don Juan pursues woman after woman, acting out fantasy after fantasy. Yet, regardless of how sensuously satisfying the sexual experience might be, he remains unfulfilled. Focusing only on his own sexual needs, Don Juan is left empty and alone.

Many of us have mistaken Don Juan for a romantic hero rather than the tragic figure that he is. We fail to recognize that while the drama of seduction is a natural part of human nature, for it to have meaning for both the seducer and the seduced it must involve the entire beings of both. Unfortunately, lust is impatient, unwilling to devote the time or energy into caring, sharing, and commitment to mutual satisfaction and meaning. So it continues isolated and alone.

We need not look only to classic literature for examples of the lonely nature of lust. We have been surrounded by them for years in our own culture: pornographic magazines and films, bars with "adult entertainment." "The Business of Porn," an article in the *U.S. News and World Report* (February 10, 1997), reported some staggering pornography statistics. It stated that in 1996 Americans spent more than $8 billion on sex magazines, computer porn, adult cable programming, peep shows, live sex acts, hard-core videos, and sexual devices. Between $750 million and $1 billion were spent on telephone sex.

This is the face of lust which we label pornography. It is the sexual desire that seeks only self-gratification rather than deep personal communion. In the Fall 1982 issue of *Leadership* magazine, an anonymous minister wrote of his own descent into hell through lust. He confessed a ten-year bondage which disrupted, and almost destroyed, his relationship with his wife and God. His lust led him down a lonely path of pornographic pleasure—from magazines to movies to live sex shows. If cyberspace pornography had been available then, he could have kept on his lonely, destructive path of lust without risking his clergy reputation by being seen at a live sex show.

By its very nature, pornography is a lonely path of lust which cannot arrive at a destination of satisfaction. It can only quench our senses for a season. As lust moves its captive from one pornographic perversion to another, the senses are numbed and more bizarre experiences are sought for satisfaction.

Our Christian opposition to pornography is not a puritanical sexual rigidity. Nor can the church allow herself to be deterred in her opposition to the pornography industry by accusations of censoring free speech and artistic expression. Just because persons do not believe themselves to be manipulated or exploited does not mean that they and others are *not* being manipulated and exploited. When we live in community with one another, responsibilities often outweigh rights. Therefore an individual's right to artistic self-expression may not outweigh that person's responsibility to contribute to the common good of avoiding exploitation in our society. The social consequence of lust-run-wild is human exploitation at its worst. This exploitation sustains an illegal underground economy that connects hard-core pornography, prostitution, and drugs. Fifty years from now, even the secular historians will be asking how a citizenry committed to "the common good" could tolerate such a deadly enterprise. And certainly God will judge us Christians for being so unconcerned and irresponsible.

Reflecting and Recording

Only in a mutual, permanent commitment in the same direction—a relationship of sexual and emotional fidelity—can love that becomes "one flesh" be nurtured. The United Methodist Church states the biblical and Christian understanding of sexual expression in this formula: *fidelity in marriage, celibacy in singleness.* Do you agree with this formula? Do the members of your church agree? Spend some time in self-examination around this formula.

■ ■ ■

Is there a person in your family or circle of friends who has suffered because this formula was disregarded?

■ ■ ■

Have you been personally hurt or felt violated because this formula was disregarded? Make enough notes here to get in touch with that experience.

Do you have a lust problem that is leading to the use of pornography? Are you drawn more and more to television and movies that feature explicit sex? Do you find yourself daydreaming about illicit sexual encounters?

■ ■ ■

Is there a pornography problem in your community to which you and your church need to give attention?

■ ■ ■

During the Day

Do you need to talk to a pastor or counselor about your sexual fantasies? If so, make an appointment today.

Find the opportunity to talk to someone about the pornography industry in your community. Express your concern and explore ways to make a witness and express opposition.

DAY 6

Good News—Bad News

The good news is that in Creation, God made us male and female. Our sexuality is a precious gift of God. Both for biological reasons—that humankind may continue—and for the fulfillment of creative purpose and meaning, the deepest love and *knowing* a man and woman can know. Male and female are designed for sexual union. The basic expression of that union, sexual intercourse, is a deeply pleasurable act. In that physical union, man and woman give and receive profound enjoyment and fulfillment.

The bad news is that, since the Fall and our bondage to self, we turn this gracious gift of God's creative love into occasions for selfishness, power seeking, greed, and self-centered lust. As indicated in Day 2 of this week, Paul makes the case that uncontrolled lust is one of the most blatant signs of our sinfulness and our refusal to honor God. He also connects the sin of lust and sexual deviation with all sorts of deadly expressions of a "debased mind."

> For this reason God gave them up to degrading passions. Their women exchanged natural intercourse for unnatural, and in the same way also the men, giving up natural intercourse with women, were consumed with passion for one another. Men committed shameless acts with men and received in their own persons the due penalty for their error.
>
> And since they did not see fit to acknowledge God, God gave them up to a debased mind and to things that should not be done. They were filled with every kind of wickedness, evil, covetousness, malice. Full of envy, murder, strife, deceit, craftiness, they are gossips, slanderers, God-haters, insolent, haughty, boastful, inventors of evil, rebellious toward parents, foolish, faithless, heartless, ruthless. They know God's

decree, that those who practice such things deserve to die—yet they not only do them but even applaud others who practice them.

—Romans 1:26-32

Promiscuity is what the Bible calls "fornication" and what today is often referred to as "casual" sex. Instead of liberating all, the sexual revolution has imprisoned many. Sexual freedom became an ideology that began to blossom into sexual license in the sixties. It was connected with the protest culture, the human potential movement, the psychology of self-expression and self-actualization. "You do your thing and I'll do mine" for "I'm OK and you're OK." The barrier to human fulfillment and meaning was all the moral and spiritual constraints that had been laid upon us. The sooner we could rid ourselves of those constraints the happier we would be.

Our culture became so sexually permissive that we could teach our children all about the "mechanics" of sex, exhort them to play it safe with sex, and provide them condoms to be safe. But we couldn't—and still can't—seem to raise the moral issue or introduce the spiritual dynamic of *knowing* as the heart of the sexual relationship. We have been too slow in recognizing the sexual revolution for what it is—the great destroyer of the family structure of society. Only in light of the controversy of abortion and the grave threat of the AIDS epidemic has it become permissible to talk about abstinence in the sex education classes of our public schools.

The very fact that we use the word *casual* to describe the deepest, most profound and pleasurable physical experience for which male and female were created is indicative of how lust has done its deadly work on the broad social fabric of our life. Lust is sexual desire apart from commitment and responsibility. We have so trivialized sex that it can have little or nothing to do with love and affection or even elementary human caring.

Adultery is lust's work of temptation and allurement for married persons. There is a story of Moses coming down from the mountain with two tablets. "The good news," he said, "is that we were able to hold God to only ten commandments. The bad news is that *adultery is still there*."

To that story we can say that adultery is not wrong simply because it is one of God's Ten Commandments. God commanded against adultery because it is wrong. "Thou shalt not commit adultery" is good, not bad, news. Marriage and family is God's idea—two people bound together in fidelity and trust, "knowing" each other in the depth of sexual oneness and producing children for the continuation of the race—it is God's pinnacle of intention and creation. Lust's ugly face of adultery is an archenemy of marriage and family. It is in a covenant of faithfulness and permanence that love can grow to maturity and sex can become more than the satisfaction of an "animal" need.

The practice of homosexual sex can be another expression of lust and sexual need. Scripture and the tradition of the church have witnessed that "the practice of homosexuality . . . is incompatible with Christian teaching." While God did not limit the full meaning of sex to procreation, reason certainly shows that the continuation of the human race was one of God's primary purposes in creating us as sexual beings and distinctively male and female. Reason can also show, then, that homosexual sex conflicts with the biblical account of the ways males and females are created and denies the procreative purpose.

The sexual revolution has made it possible for champions of the practice of homosexuality to turn it into a "justice" (human-rights) issue, making it difficult in the secular arena and sometimes even in the church to raise the moral and spiritual dimensions of the issue. There is indeed a justice element in the issue of homosexuality. Anytime persons are discriminated against or suffer violence and injury because of hateful attitudes against them, justice is at stake. However, relegating this highly charged issue to the arena of social justice overlooks its complexity and ignores the difficult and oftentimes painful moral-spiritual questions.

We confessed on Day 1 of this week that the church has been at its harshest and most unforgiving when dealing with the sins of lust, particularly sexual lust. This violates the life and teaching of Christ, the "head" of the church. We must not be judgmental and unforgiving in our attitude toward sinners. We, too, are sinful. We may judge sin and speak prophetically of its destructiveness in our life and of its violation of Kingdom values. But our prophetic speaking, our moral teaching, and our efforts at reformation must be in the context of love and forgiveness and renewal.

We don't have clear evidence about what causes a propensity to homosexuality. It does seem that some people are influenced by forces they did not choose and cannot control. We also know that feeding the sexual instinct can become a substitute for other ravaging and unfulfilled desires. We have discovered, too, that promiscuity is often an expression of a person's search for love, appreciation, security, and belonging. Only God knows all the factors that have made us what we are. God is a merciful judge, and we can be no less.

When we turn the scrutiny toward ourselves rather than others, we have to claim the freedom we have in all sexual matters. What we do with our lust is a choice—a matter of will. The discipline of our will and a cultivated willingness to forego immediate gratification for a larger good and more lasting joy is the antidote for lust and the misdirection of our sexual needs.

Reflecting and Recording

Consider the following experiences:

(1) A twenty-seven-year-old unmarried woman had an abortion when she was ten weeks pregnant. She knew who the father was, but he was not the person she wanted to marry, and having a child would disrupt her professional career path. She is the daughter of one of your friends.

(2) A forty-five-year-old man and his forty-two-year-old wife have three children: a twenty-one-year-old, a nineteen-year-old, and a fifteen-year-old. The husband made it clear when they married that he wanted his wife to "stay at home with the children" and she was quite happy with that. She has discovered that he is having an affair that has been going on for at least four years. The couple are your best friends, and she has shared her discovery with you.

(3) Your son has been bringing his college roommate, John, home rather frequently for two years. John has become a close friend of the family. Your son tells you that he has suspected it, and now he is sure: He returned to campus Saturday evening rather than Sunday as he planned and discovered John and another man having sex in their room.

Be honest now in assessing your feelings. If these were actual personal experiences, which would bother you most? Why?

■ ■ ■

Spend some time thinking about these questions:

Look at your own life. Have you ever felt used and/or abused sexually? What is your most negative, painful, destructive experience, resulting from lust and the misdirection of sexual need?

Do you need to share this experience with a pastor or counselor?

Has your lust made you abusive of another? Have you used another simply to satisfy your need? Has the way you treated another sexually made him or her feel like a "thing" rather than a person?

Do you need to ask forgiveness from another person whom you have mistreated and hurt sexually?

■ ■ ■

During the Day

Follow through in action or any decision you have made or any direction you need to take as a result of your reflection.

DAY 7

"Neither Do I Condemn You"

The scribes and the Pharisees brought a woman who had been caught in adultery; and making her stand before all of them, they said to [Jesus], "Teacher, this woman was caught in the very act of committing adultery. Now in the law Moses commanded us to stone such women. Now what do you say?" They said this to test him, so that they might have some charge to bring against him. Jesus bent down and wrote with his finger on the ground. When they kept on questioning him, he straightened up and said to them, "Let anyone among you who is without sin be the first to throw a stone at her." And once again he bent down and wrote on the ground. When they heard it, they went away, one by one, beginning with the elders; and Jesus was left alone with the woman standing before him. Jesus straightened up and said to her, "Woman, where are they?

Has no one condemned you?" She said, "No one, sir." And Jesus said, "Neither do I condemn you. Go your way, and from now on do not sin again."

—John 8:3-11

This story is revealing, not alone in that it is a clear expression of the forgiving mercy of Jesus: the pardon of grace. It is also a picture of the power of grace. As we emphasized on Day 7 of Week One, pardon and power go together.

Pardon: "Neither do I condemn you."

Power: "Go your way, and from now on do not sin again."

The grace of Christ accepts us where we are but it does not leave us as we are. What distinguishes the behavior of the "new person in Christ" from the unconverted person is this: The Christian seeks the power of Christ to express wholeness in love rather than surrendering to the passion of lust. The Christian forgives and receives forgiveness, but also lives under the demand of a Christlike model for humanity.

The deepest insights of psychology have taught us that the most successful recipe for a happy and fulfilled life is to lose oneself in something greater than oneself. Yet we often discover that conscious efforts in the direction of self-seeking are strangely self-frustrating. Ambition costs us friends; power corrupts those who wield it; wealth brings the curse of Midas; sexual excess ends in secret disgust. This should come as no surprise to the followers of Jesus, who taught them, "Those who want to save their life will lose it, and those who lose their life for my sake will find it" (Matt. 16:25).

Becoming Christian means that we give Christ the freedom to live in us and transform us into new persons. Lust, then, must be driven from our awareness. This is a process, not a *fait accompli*. We immerse ourselves in God's word, the Bible; we discipline ourselves in prayer; we open ourselves through daily and hourly commitment to the presence of the living Christ, and we consciously and constantly surrender ourselves to the shaping power of Christ. Our love is flavored by the Savior's love and gradually, but certainly, love becomes dominant in place of the "lusts of the flesh" which would otherwise control and destroy us.

In this overall context of commitment and surrender to Christ, we take specific steps:

One, we make a solid determination to be free of lust and believe that Christ is able and willing to assist us in our victory. Being free in Christ means having the freedom to say no to lust.

Two, we keep a healthy, holy perspective about our bodies—we guard against indulging our bodies, but we refuse to despise them, believing that our bodies are the temple of the Holy Spirit.

Three, we never lose sight of the fact that sex is sacred; it is God's gift to us.

Reflecting and Recording

What is a moral concern for which you need the power of grace—some habit you need to break, some addiction that is controlling you? Name it in one sentence.

Spend the rest of your time reflecting on specific steps to prevent lust from controlling you.

During the Day

Make plans to attend your group meeting today. Is there anyone in the group who has special needs to which you need to respond?

Whether in a group or not, are there persons you know who would profit from using this workbook? Make plans today to see them, to share what this workbook has meant to you, and ask if they would be willing for you to provide them a copy.

Group Meeting for Week Seven

You may have begun your discussion last week about possibilities for your group continuing to meet. We would suggest two possibilities. One, you could select two or three weeks of the workbook that were especially difficult or meaningful. Go through those weeks as an extension of your time together.

Two, you could decide that you are going to continue your group, using another resource. You may appoint two or three persons to bring a resource suggestion to the group next week.

Another possibility is for one or two persons to decide they will recruit and lead a group of persons through this workbook. Many people are looking for a small-group experience, and this is a way to respond to their need.

Sharing Together

1. Begin your sharing by allowing each person to share his/her most meaningful and most difficult days of this week's involvement with the workbook.
2. Spend eight to twelve minutes sharing your experience of how the church, as you have known it, has dealt with sex—the role the church has played in your understanding of human sexuality.
3. Spend eight to twelve minutes discussing lust as preoccupation with objects of our desire, other than sex.
4. Acknowledging the difficulty and knowing that most—maybe all—will not be able to share, is anyone in the group able to tell about pain and brokenness caused by any of the following expressions of lust: pornography, adultery, promiscuity.
5. On Day 6, in Reflecting and Recording (page 154), three experiences were suggested. Review those three experiences and spend eight to ten minutes discussing how you would feel if these were actual personal experiences. Which would bother you most and why?
6. Spend ten to fifteen minutes discussing these three assertions: (1) Love treats people as persons; lust treats them as things; (2) Lust is not interested in commitment; and (3) Marriage is a necessary ingredient for lasting love.
7. Spend four to six minutes discussing your and your congregation's response to the biblical mandate that can be expressed as "fidelity in marriage, celibacy in singleness."

8. Spend six to eight minutes discussing how individuals and the church can hold to strict moral values and yet be loving and forgiving of those who break God's laws.
9. Consider this statement: The grace of Christ accepts us where we are but it does not leave us as we are. Spend five to ten minutes discussing how you would have to change personally, and how your church would have to change, if you really believed that.
10. Spend the balance of your sharing time discussing the notion that our bodies are "temples of the Holy Spirit" and the assertion that the sin of lust is a good which has somehow become misdirected.

Praying Together

1. There is a lot of pain and hurt in many of our lives as a result of the misuse and perversion of sex; likewise a lot of pain results from our lust, unrelated to sex. There is also the pain of divorce and broken families. Take some time to allow persons to share their pain. Persons may not be able to tell their story—only to verbalize enough to designate the pain and hurt. Listen carefully to the sharing so you can be specific in your praying.
2. When all have shared, enter into a season of spontaneous prayer. Everyone who wishes can offer verbal prayer. Make sure that everyone who shares pain and hurt is specifically prayed for by name.
3. Close your time singing together a familiar hymn or chorus.

Week Eight

Gluttony
Misplaced Hunger

DAY 1

Gluttony: Twin Brother to Lust

Last week, in our consideration of lust, we focused a great deal on the body and its pleasures. How we perceive our bodies, how we use, disuse, and abuse them, is a key to understanding and dealing with sin. On Day 3 of last week we called attention to Paul's marvelous image of the body as a "temple of the Holy Spirit" and his call to use our bodies "for God's glory." That image and call are more powerful when set in the larger context of Paul's teaching:

> "All things are lawful for me," but not all things are beneficial. "All things are lawful for me," but I will not be dominated by anything. "Food is meant for the stomach and the stomach for food," and God will destroy both one and the other. The body is meant not for fornication but for the Lord, and the Lord for the body. And God raised the Lord and will also raise us by his power. Do you not know that your bodies are members of Christ? Should I therefore take the members of Christ and make them members of a prostitute? Never! Do you not know that whoever is united to a prostitute becomes one body with her? For it is said, "The two shall be one flesh." But anyone united to the Lord becomes one spirit with him. Shun fornication! Every sin that a person commits is outside the body; but the fornicator sins against the body itself. Or do you not know that your body is a temple of the Holy Spirit within you, which you have from God, and that you are not your own? For you were bought with a price; therefore glorify God in your body.
>
> —1 Corinthians 6:12-20

"The body is meant . . . for the Lord, and the Lord for the body. . . . glorify God in your body" (vv. 13 and 20). Paul centers on fornication (promiscuity—carnal sin), but he mentions food and the stomach in the same breath as he is condemning fornication as a sin "against the body itself."

So, this week we take a long look at the seventh deadly sin: gluttony. Gluttony is a twin brother to lust because it has many of the same characteristics. It is a misplaced hunger. As lust, according to Frederick Buechner, is the "craving for salt of a person who is dying of thirst," gluttony is the mad pursuit of the bodily pleasures that never completely satisfy. We connect it with the craving for food and this has been its primary expression. But the person who drinks or smokes too much is as gluttonous as the person who overeats. As Richard Holloway reminds us, we can take it farther than that.

> The person who talks too much, the compulsive prattler who invades our quietness and space with voracious and uninterruptible talk, is as much a glutton as the person who can't stop eating. Lust and gluttony share many characteristics, but their main agreement lies in this: they have lost all balance and proportion. They do not see the natural appetites as instincts that have to be balanced by other considerations; instead, they allow them a disproportionate role, and they can end by dominating and controlling the whole personality. The full tragedy lies in the fact that, at the end, the gluttonous and the lustful are deprived of the pleasures that once ensnared them. The drunkard is driven by a dominating compulsion that lacks all pleasure, and he often ends by seeking oblivion from the torment.
>
> —Holloway, pp. 35–36

Reflecting and Recording

Who is the most gluttonous person you know? Spend a moment locating that person in your thoughts.

■ ■ ■

Is he/she an overeater, an indulgent drinker or smoker, or a person in whom some other bodily appetite has run wild? Do you know anything about his/her needs? What may be driving him/her to gluttony? Now write a brief description of the person, keeping in mind some of these questions.

Now think—who is the most lustful person you know? Go through the same process suggested above, get that person clearly in your thoughts, and write a description of him/her.

Spend a bit of time now comparing the two persons you have described. Do these persons demonstrate the claim that gluttony is a twin brother to lust?

■ ■ ■

During the Day

Pay attention to your desires, particularly your bodily desires for food and sex. Do these desires reflect other needs in your life?

DAY 2

Eating to Live Or Living to Eat

Brothers and sisters, join in imitating me, and observe those who live according to the example you have in us. For many live as enemies of the cross of Christ; I have often told you of them, and now I tell you even with tears. Their end is destruction; their god is the belly; and their glory is in their shame; their minds are set on earthly things. But our citizenship is in heaven, and it is from there that we are expecting a Savior, the Lord Jesus Christ. He will transform the body of our humiliation that it may be conformed to the body of his glory, by the power that also enables him to make all things subject to himself.

—Philippians 3:17-21

Paul is a bold man. He does not say to the Philippians, as most modern preachers would say, "Don't do as I do, but do as I say." Rather, as Joseph Barber Lightfoot has translated verse 17: "Vie with others in imitating me." The New Revised Standard Version, quoted above, puts it, "join in imitating me." Paul could be bold because he was living such a disciplined moral and spiritual life that he could, without pride, and certainly in a way that he could not be accused of vain arrogance, invite people to follow his example.

His boldness extends throughout this passage. He minces no words in addressing the people in the church at Philippi whose conduct was an open scandal. "Their end is destruction; their god is the belly; and their glory is in their shame; their minds are set on earthly things" (v. 19). Is there a more graphic description of gluttony? The gluttonous allow their belly to become their god—paying homage to their appetites, their lust and greed, conspicuous consumption being their extravagant act of praise.

To talk about our belly being our god may be inelegant, but we need something to get and sustain our attention about the sin of gluttony. Our intemperate desires and our self-indulgence mark us as people of shame, with minds set on earthly things, and Paul is right: our "end is destruction." Too many of us no longer eat to live, we live to eat. That formula means more than stuffing ourselves with food. It means the excess consumption of food, drink, drugs, cigarettes, but also the gadgets and things that are offered to satisfy all our desires. No building contractor would think of building a house to be sold on the open market with only one garage. We have come a long way from President Herbert Hoover's promise in the early 1930s of a chicken in every pot. A credit-card society has virtually put an end to delayed gratification. We have become a people who claim instant gratification as a self-evident right.

When we talk about gluttony this week, we are talking about the consumption of food—but more, we are talking primarily about self-indulgence. We are not addressing the issue of overweight and obesity. We know there are complex chemical factors in our bodily makeup, and that there are many people who cannot control their weight simply by consuming less food. Most obese people despise their weight and suffer emotionally, relationally, spiritually because of their craving for food and their tendency to always overeat. Nutritional scientists are not in agreement on why people crave particular foods, and often the wrong foods, for their insatiable appetite. They do agree that chemical imbalances, whatever the case, are not the willful decision of the victims of obesity. We do know that self-indulgence, especially with food, alcohol, and tobacco, creates chemical imbalances that turn us into addicts.

According to *Alcohol Health and Research World*, in 1994 almost 13.8 million Americans had problems with alcohol. Far more than that have a food problem. The two biggest sellers in bookstores are cookbooks and diet books. The cookbooks tell us how to cook delicious foods; the diet books tell us how not to eat them. These two major addictions are connected with gluttony, overindulgence. Gluttony is living to "eat, drink, and be merry." So we can be gluttonous with food, alcohol, cigarettes, and sex, but also with virtually anything—shopping, work, soap operas, exercise, video games, gambling, computers.

I moved to Wilmore, Kentucky, in July 1994 to become the president of Asbury Theological Seminary. Southland Christian Church, one of the most dynamic congregations in the nation, is between Wilmore and Lexington, about five miles from where I live. I had heard of this congregation and their senior minister, Wayne B. Smith. I wanted to attend their church and hear Wayne preach before my wife and I settled into the local United Methodist congregation.

The Sunday I attended, the last Sunday in August, Wayne was preaching on lust as a part of a series on the seven deadly sins. It was an outstanding sermon. I was intrigued by Wayne's announcement that he would preach the last sermon in the series the next Sunday. He had saved it for that weekend since it was Labor Day weekend and attendance would be down. The people of the congregation, who knew and loved their preacher, began to laugh as he completed his announcement by saying he would preach on gluttony.

Wayne weighed 265 pounds and his people knew that weight was a constant battle for him. I didn't get to hear his sermon in person but I requested an audiotape and listened to it. He could not say with Paul, "Imitate me . . . follow my example," and he confessed that. Wayne demonstrated a very healthy sense of humor as he told this story in the sermon:

> My secretary received a phone call. The caller said, "I would like to speak with the head hog." She said, "I know Wayne is overweight but no one has ever been that disrespectful." "Well," he said, "let me apologize. I'm a hog farmer over in Scott County. I raise hogs and I just sold some of them for $5,000. I watch Wayne on television and I really

like him. I don't go to church anywhere. I thought I might send $500 to Southland Christian Church." She said, "Just a minute—I think the big pig just walked in."

But Wayne did not hide behind that sense of humor.

Does being 120 pounds overweight bother me? Yes, mentally and spiritually. Does it hurt my witness? Of course it does! It's hard to sell a product you do not use and a religion that you do not live. Am I a hypocrite? Yes. How can I preach if I'm a hypocrite? If only the perfect bird sang in the forest, it would be quiet there. If only perfect preachers stood in the pulpit, we would not have a message. All have sinned and fallen short of the glory of God. Is that an excuse? No, it is a statement of guilt and also why I'm preaching.

That's the honesty we need, for we are all guilty in one way or another—guilty of gluttony, the overindulgence that affects our physical health, inhibits our performance, separates us from others, and blocks our relationship with God.

Reflecting and Recording

We mentioned above that we can be gluttonous with shopping, work, soap operas, exercise, video games, gambling, and computers as well as with food, alcohol, cigarettes, and sex. How do you respond to this suggestion?

■ ■ ■

What would you add to our list with which we can be gluttonous? Name them here:

Paul wrote that the god of the Philippians was their belly. He was talking about gluttony, overindulgence. Name three areas in your life where you are tempted to overindulge.

In his word to the Philippians, Paul said that we Christians are "citizens of heaven." If you stayed in constant awareness of that fact—that as a Christian you are a citizen of heaven—could you deal better with those areas of your life where you are tempted to overindulge?

■ ■ ■

Close your time reflecting on this word of Paul, Philippians 3:21, and claiming the promise and power of it. *Good News Translation* makes this verse plain: The Lord Jesus Christ "will change our weak mortal bodies and make them like his own glorious body, using that power by which he is able to bring all things under his rule."

■ ■ ■

During the Day

Both lust and gluttony are connected with our bodies and our bodily appetites. The body is the temple of the Holy Spirit, but for that to be fully actualized we must surrender ourselves to Christ, allowing him to be Lord of our bodies. Philippians 3:21, with which you closed your reflection time, is printed on page 185. Cut it out and put it in a place like the refrigerator door, bathroom mirror, or instrument panel of your car, where you will see it often. Immerse yourself in the truth of it, and let it be a call to yield all your hungers, thirsts, desires, and needs to Christ.

DAY 3

Trying to Feed the Soul with the Body's Food

Last week we focused on lust. We did not deal explicitly with the fact that our society is saturated with sex. The most pervasive ingredient in advertising is sex. Everything from toothpaste to automobiles is sold by appealing to lust.

Why? We believe it is the surest sign of the inner emptiness of our age, and the imperative need of every human being to find meaning and satisfaction in life. Sex is offered as the answer. In our experience of counseling as pastors, we have discovered that persons turn to lust because of boredom. The French have a word for it—*ennui. The American Heritage Dictionary* describes *ennui* as "listlessness and dissatisfaction resulting from lack of interest; boredom."

Persons, male and female, have affairs when they feel that life has become flat, without excitement; they are unable to make positive and meaningful use of leisure. We have noted that many women have affairs, or turn to alcohol and drugs, when they have everything. Their husbands provide them all the "things" of success, but do not give them the attention, affirmation, and intimacy needed for fulfillment and meaning. So they seek attention, affirmation, and intimacy with another. Interestingly, in our experience, men most often have affairs either when they are at the top rung of success, or when they feel themselves as failures. Their success does not provide the satisfaction it promised—so they look for another "conquest." Or, their power gives them the distorted notion that they deserve whatever they desire. On the failure side, they look for a way to prove their worth.

The "middle-aged fling" is a common expression of people looking for adventure, excitement—something that has eluded them in any quality, consistent, and ongoing way. All of these expressions are efforts at filling the emptiness, the vacuum—overcoming the flatness of existence. It is our effort to feed the soul with the body's food.

This is the underlying sin of gluttony as well as lust and greed: seeking to feed the soul with the body's food. There is a revealing line in Paul's teaching about eating food sacrificed to idols:

> Now concerning food sacrificed to idols: we know that "all of us possess knowledge." Knowledge puffs up, but love builds up. Anyone who claims to know something does not yet have the necessary knowledge; but anyone who loves God is known by him. Hence, as to the eating of food offered to idols, we know that "no idol in the world really exists," and that "there is no God but one." Indeed, even though there may be so-called gods in heaven or on earth—as in fact there are many gods and many lords— yet for us there is one God, the Father, from whom are all things and for whom we exist, and one Lord, Jesus Christ, through whom are all things and through whom we exist. It is not everyone, however, who has this knowledge. Since some have become so accustomed to idols until now, they still think of the food they eat as food offered to an idol; and their conscience, being weak, is defiled. "Food will not bring us close to God." We are no worse off if we do not eat, and no better off if we do. But take care that this liberty of yours does not somehow become a stumbling block to the weak. For if others see you, who possess knowledge, eating in the temple of an idol, might they not, since their conscience is weak, be encouraged to the point of eating food sacrificed to idols? So by your knowledge those weak believers for whom Christ died are destroyed. But when you thus sin against members of your family, and wound their conscience when it is weak, you sin against Christ. Therefore, if food is a cause of their falling, I will never eat meat, so that I may not cause one of them to fall.
>
> —1 Corinthians 8:1-13

"Food will not bring us close to God" (v. 8), nor will the feeding of any of our instincts, tastes, and passions. Where food is concerned, we are in a double bind as a part of American culture. We are constantly bombarded with the call of advertisers to eat sumptuously. At the same time we are told that for health's and image's sake we must be thin.

There is a story of a woman who had tried everything to lose weight—diet, exercise, appetite-suppressing pills. Finally she found something that worked. She attached a 12" x 16" picture of a beautiful, thin, shapely woman, dressed in a bikini, on her refrigerator door. Every time she was tempted to snack, the picture of what she might become was a powerful deterrent. During the first month she lost ten pounds—but her husband gained twenty!

We are in a double bind. Along with sex, the most prominent imaging in advertising is eating and drinking. We can't escape the onslaught. Yet, the images of health, beauty, and success are the glamorous woman, about twenty pounds underweight, and the lithe, lean man with no bulges anywhere. New cookbooks, with exotic menus and the ways of charming entertainment, compete with the newest best-seller which guarantees a sure and healthy diet to lose weight.

Paul was not addressing the double bind in which we find ourselves, but his word is a saving lesson: "Food will not bring us close to God." There are only a few people who don't need this message. Food is not the answer. Fat will not condemn you, nor will thin save you. "There is . . . no condemnation for those [fat or thin] who are in Christ Jesus" (Rom. 8:1). What we weigh, or the shape of our body, is of no account in our relationship to Christ. We are loved and accepted by Christ. Paul said that we are saved by grace and not good works: "For by grace you have been saved through faith, and this is not your own doing; it is the gift of God—not the result of works, so that no one may boast" (Eph. 2:8). Need we add for clarity: We are saved by faith, not by diet?

In Sam Keen's book *Inward Bound*, he is convinced that boredom is epidemic but we will not live with our boredom long enough to experience our emptiness and begin to discover meaning. He says that boredom is the "symptom of our successful failure" and entertainment, the quest for excitement, replaces deep satisfaction. "We buy and consume to fill the emptiness and give us a sense of worth." Bored persons numb themselves and those around them.

> Once the nerve of feeling has been deadened, the bored person seeks some stimulation that will give him or her a sense of being alive. Diversion, entertainment, sensory titillation are supposed to compensate for the surrendered sense of feeling fulness. Quite often, the inner emptiness leads to an exaggerated sense of hunger and addition. Obsessive eating, drinking, smoking, consuming are the most common ways of trying to fill the inner void.
>
> —Keen, p. 94

This obsessive consumption is the futile effort of trying to feed the soul with the body's food. When will we heed the call of Jesus:

> Therefore do not worry, saying, "What will we eat?" or "What will we drink?" or "What will we wear?" For it is the Gentiles who strive for all these things; and indeed your heavenly Father knows that you need all these things. But strive first for the kingdom of God and his righteousness, and all these things will be given to you as well.
>
> —Matthew 6:31-33

Reflecting and Recording

Go back and read what you wrote about the gluttonous and lustful persons in your reflecting and recording on Day 1. Were any of these, as you know them, trying to feed his or her soul with the body's food?

■ ■ ■

As we mentioned earlier, persons turn to lust because of boredom; women often turn to alcohol and drugs when they have everything money can buy, but don't have attention, affirmation, and intimacy. Men have affairs at the height of success, but also in their failure. Do you know a person who has had an affair or has a drinking problem? Give thought to why they may have sought satisfaction in this fashion.

■ ■ ■

Spend some time in honest self-examination. What are your feelings about your body? Do you feel guilty? anxious? determined?

■ ■ ■

Write a brief prayer expressing your feelings and decisions flowing out of these reflections.

During the Day

Continue immersing yourself in the scripture you cut out yesterday.

DAY 4

The Body—A Servant of the Mind and the Spirit

Saint Francis of Assisi referred to his body as "Brother Ass." It was his playful way of saying that the body is to be a servant of the mind and the spirit.

As a brother, the body is not ignored or scorned. It deserves attention, even a degree of reverence, but it is to be the servant of our minds and souls, not our master. How can we as Christians maintain a balanced view regarding our bodies?

An extreme asceticism is not the answer. At different periods in church history and by varying groups, an erroneous theology of the body has been championed. The body has been seen as bad, evil, even demonic. In this understanding, not only must we numb ourselves to the body's appetites, instincts, and needs, we must punish our bodies. Extreme expressions of this theology were starvation—long, long periods of denying the body food—and flagellation—lacerating oneself with a whip. This was a part of ascetic practice primarily in monastic communities. It not only involved flagellation, but also such practices as dropping burning wax on the skin, inviting the bite of insects, and wearing hair shirts. It was an effort to bring "Brother Ass" under total submission, but it was also a distorted notion of self-punishment for sinful thoughts and attitudes, an effort to "prove" submission to the Lord.

This is a false caricature of healthy spiritual discipline. Though Jesus was the most spiritually disciplined person we know, though he was an ascetic in terms of self-denial, extreme asceticism would be as repulsive to Jesus as to us. This is the way Jesus presented himself:

> But to what will I compare this generation? It is like children sitting in the marketplaces and calling to one another, "We played the flute for you, and you did not dance; we wailed, and you did not mourn." For John came neither eating nor drinking, and they say, "He has a demon"; the Son of Man came eating and drinking, and they say, "Look, a glutton and a drunkard, a friend of tax collectors and sinners!" Yet wisdom is vindicated by her deeds.
>
> —Matthew 11:16-19

Obsessive preoccupation with health can be a form of asceticism. For instance, we become health food addicts and as rigidly fundamental in our dieting as a religious fundamentalist may be about doctrine. Our interest in eating can also become a form of gluttony. Henry Fairlie gives us a word picture of obsessive dieters:

> They are constantly going to their refrigerators, perhaps more than anyone else, even when it is not yet time for their rations, counting what is there, making sure that not one item is missing of what has become so precious to them. They gaze on the morsels, fondle them, even rearrange them, each in its sack, all lovingly known and enumerated. From hour to hour they return to make an inventory. When in *extremis*, they count the spinach leaves. But at last the bell rings. It is mealtime. Salivating like Pavlov's dogs, they scurry to the kitchen table with a stick of celery, a radish, a spoonful of cottage cheese, and a dried apricot for dessert. Watch them as they eat. They devour their delicacies just as the conventional glutton sucks up his bouillabaisse. Their eyes also are fixed on their plates.
>
> They occupy the rest of their days by reading and thinking about food. There must be some new regimen that they should be following, one more impurity that has been discovered in the endive. Whether they are eating or not, their minds are on their food and what their food is doing to their bodies. (Their obsession with it is destroying their minds, but that does not bother them.)
>
> —Fairlie, pp. 163–164

While gluttony does have to do with overindulgence, stuffing our bodies with food we do not need and using and consuming "things" in a voracious, irresponsible way, it also has to do with *preoccupation*. In this sense it is not only a twin brother to lust, it is at least a first cousin to sloth. Like sloth it disconnects us from those around us. The most obvious expression of this disconnection is overfed people ignoring the needs of the poor, undernourished children in their own neighborhoods and starving people around the world.

Reflecting and Recording

Is there anything about which you are obsessively preoccupied? You think about it all the time. Your thinking about it interrupts other involvement, demands attention that should be placed elsewhere, drains you of energy you could be giving to other persons or activities. Name that preoccupation in one sentence.

Now write a paragraph describing how this obsessive preoccupation is affecting your life.

Spend three or four minutes thinking about what you are going to do about your obsessive preoccupation.

■ ■ ■

Spend the balance of your time reflecting on how you feel about and how you treat your body. What changes do you need to make to be able, with Saint Francis, to see your body as "Brother Ass"?

■ ■ ■

During the Day

Be observant of the demands your body—its instincts, desires, appetites, needs—makes of you today. How do these fit into your obsessive preoccupation or your body being "Brother Ass"?

DAY 5

Feasting Is Not Gluttony

Gluttony, like most all sins, is a perversion of something that is good and right. Eating and drinking are essential in life. It should not surprise us, then, that food and drink receive a good bit of attention in all religious faiths. Sacred meals, food regulations, and dietary laws are common and integrated into religious practice.

In consideration of the sin of gluttony, we need then to talk about feasting and fasting. For the most part, we have lost the religious meaning of both. In the Judeo-Christian tradition, feasts have special meaning. The people of Israel were always feasting. Their feasts began as particular celebrations of thanksgiving for what God had done. Abraham gave a feast to celebrate God's intervention in his life. He and his wife, Sarah, were far beyond childbearing years, but God blessed them with a son, Isaac. When Isaac was old enough to be weaned from his mother's milk, Abraham gave a great feast. (See Genesis 21:8.)

Some feasts which began as a particular celebration became institutionalized as ongoing rituals of the people. The paramount one in Jewish life, in which one of the two sacraments in Protestant Christianity is rooted, is the Feast of the Passover. This feast was held on the night that God delivered Israel from captivity in Egypt. It was a feast of unleavened bread and a "lamb without blemish." The blood of the slain lamb was sprinkled on the doorposts and lintel of those who were feasting as an identifying mark, so that the angel of death would pass over and not claim the firstborn in those homes. Moses instructed the people that this feast would be an ongoing celebration:

> When the LORD brings you into the land of the Canaanites, the Hittites, the Amorites, the Hivites, and the Jebusites, which he swore to your ancestors to give you, a land flowing with milk and honey, you shall keep this observance in this month. Seven days you shall eat unleavened bread, and on the seventh day there shall be a festival to the LORD. Unleavened bread shall be eaten for seven days; no leavened bread shall be seen in your possession, and no leaven shall be seen among you in all your territory. You shall tell your child on that day, "It is because of what the LORD did for me when I came out of Egypt." It shall serve for you as a sign on your hand and as a reminder on your forehead, so that the teaching of the LORD may be on your lips; for with a strong hand the LORD brought you out of Egypt. You shall keep this ordinance at its proper time from year to year.
>
> —Exodus 13:5-10

In the Christian church we celebrate our Passover, the Lord's Supper. With the bread and wine we remember the "lamb slain from the foundation of the world" and our deliverance from the bondage of sin and death. We feast at the "Table of the Lord" and anticipate "the wedding banquet" when all God's children will share the joys of heaven at Christ's final triumph.

Feasting, celebration, is a part of our Christian faith. We need to remember this about Jesus: He not only entered into the sorrows of men and women, but into their joys as well. He was at home at wedding feasts and parties. It is a good thing to remember that the Christian faith is sociable; fellowship is at the heart of it. As E. Stanley Jones states it, "Everybody who belongs to Christ, belongs to everybody who belongs to Christ."

It is a given that food and drink are aids to fellowship. We feel most festive and filled with goodwill and openness to others when we share a meal. I'm sure this is one of the main reasons the law commanded the people of Israel to always provide food and hospitality to strangers.

If preoccupation with the desires and appetites of the body is a mark of gluttony, as we suggested yesterday, then an antidote is to focus our attention on those with whom we share our food. Our mealtimes could be the richest times of fellowship if we would be intentional in expressing genuine concern for members of our family or guests as we eat together.

Feasting with friends can be an act of gratitude as we enjoy the extravagant goodness of a loving God. When Jesus' disciples criticized a woman for pouring a costly bottle of perfume on him, Jesus praised her. There are occasions when excessive expression is a sign of deep gratitude for the love and goodness of God.

But feasting isn't gluttony. "Gluttony connects us neither with others or God. Gluttony is a solitary act that defeats rather than enhances community. Excessive eating is solitary, even if others are present. Feasting needs and builds community. Gluttony cares little for community." (White, p. 56)

Gluttony has no perspective; it is excessive and preoccupied with satisfying self. Feasting keeps perspective; it celebrates God's bounty and encourages eating with a grateful heart and sharing with others.

Reflecting and Recording

Name three "feasts" that you celebrate with your family and/or others on a regular basis.

Look at your last celebration of each of these feasts. Was there more gluttony than genuine feasting? Were there expressions of gratitude? Were "strangers" welcomed? Was there care for the "black sheep" of the family, reaching out to those who were lonely and hurting? Make some notes about each celebration, reflecting on these questions.

■ ■ ■

Look at your pattern of eating over the past two weeks. Select one occasion in which there was genuine sharing, where care and concern were expressed, where the focus was not on the food but on the persons with whom you shared it. Write a few sentences describing that occasion.

When was the last time you planned a "special meal," a feast, for the sake of reaching out in love to others?

■ ■ ■

Close your time with a prayer of thanksgiving for God's goodness, and for the opportunity you have to share God's goodness with others.

■ ■ ■

During the Day

Plan a "special meal" with someone or a number of persons who need your love and attention.

DAY 6

Fasting Cheerfully

Jesus was accustomed to feasting. He was a part of a religious tradition in which a number of feasts were annually celebrated by the community as an important part of the worship, liturgy, and fellowship.

Feasting was often perverted, such as the way some of the Corinthian Christians engaged in the Lord's Supper.

> Now in the following instructions I do not commend you, because when you come together it is not for the better but for the worse. For, to begin with, when you come together as a church, I hear that there are divisions among you; and to some extent I believe it. Indeed, there have to be factions among you, for only so will it become clear who among you are genuine. When you come together, it is not really to eat the Lord's supper. For when the time comes to eat, each of you goes ahead with your own supper, and one goes hungry and another becomes drunk. What! Do you not have homes to eat and drink in? Or do you show contempt for the church of God and humiliate those who have nothing? What should I say to you? Should I commend you? In this matter I do not commend you!
>
> —1 Corinthians 11:17-22

Fasting was also a part of Jesus' tradition. Likewise, it was often perverted. Jesus warned:

> And whenever you fast, do not look dismal, like the hypocrites, for they disfigure their faces so as to show others that they are fasting. Truly I tell you, they have received their reward. But when you fast, put oil on your head and wash your face, so that your fasting may be seen not by others but by your Father who is in secret; and your Father who sees in secret will reward you.
>
> —Matthew 6:16-18

Jesus was in the tradition of the prophets of Israel at their best. For him compassion was the true nature of God's love and grace. When Jesus thought and talked about fasting, he would certainly have remembered Isaiah's word:

> Is not this the fast that I choose: to loose the bonds of injustice, to undo the thongs of the yoke, to let the oppressed go free, and to break every yoke? Is it not to share your bread with the hungry, and bring the homeless poor into your house; when you see the naked, to cover them, and not to hide yourself from your own kin? Then your light shall break forth like the dawn, and your healing shall spring up quickly; your vindicator shall go before you, the glory of the LORD shall be your rear guard. Then you shall call, and the LORD will answer; you shall cry for help, and he will say, Here I am. If you remove the yoke from among you, the pointing of the finger, the speaking of evil, if you offer your food to the hungry and satisfy the needs of the afflicted, then your light shall rise in the darkness and your gloom be like the noonday. The LORD will guide you continually, and satisfy your needs in parched places, and make your bones strong; and you shall be like a watered garden, like a spring of water, whose waters never fail.
>
> —Isaiah 58:6-11

As a proper understanding and practice of feasting is an antidote for gluttony, so is fasting. But again, understanding is crucial. Fasting is denying ourselves food, but it is more. It is denying ourselves food as a discipline of remembering:

- remembering what food is all about,
- remembering the source of food,
- remembering how blessed we are to have it,
- remembering those who do not have it,
- remembering that "we do not live by bread alone."

John Wesley named fasting, along with prayer, scripture, the Lord's Supper, and Christian conferencing, as a primary means of grace. Of fasting he wrote, "Of all the means of grace there is scarce any concerning which men have run into greater extremes than that of . . . religious fasting."

> Some have exalted this beyond all Scripture and reason;—and others utterly disregarded it. . . . The truth lies between them both. . . . It is not the end, but it is a precious means thereto; a means which God himself has ordained, and in which therefore, when it is duly used, he [God] will surely give us his blessing. . . .
>
> Let every season, either of public or private fasting be a season of exercising all those holy affections which are implied in a broken and contrite heart. Let it be a season of devout mourning, of godly sorrow for sin . . .
>
> And with fasting let us always join fervent prayer, pouring out our whole souls before God, confessing our sins . . . , humbling ourselves . . . , laying open before him all our wants, all our guiltiness and helplessness. This is a season for enlarging our prayers, both in behalf of ourselves and of our brethren.
>
> —John Wesley, Works, V, pp. 345–360

Fasting is a means of practicing the fact that we cannot feed the spirit with the body's food. In one of his beatitudes, Jesus said, "Blessed are those who hunger and thirst for righteousness, for they will be filled" (Matt. 5:6). As we have been saying all this week, gluttony is a misplaced hunger. Fasting is an expression of "hungering and thirsting" for spiritual food. Gluttony deadens spiritual hunger, numbs our feelings for "higher things"; fasting keeps us alive to what Jesus knew— "My food is to do the will of him who sent me" (John 4:34).

Methodist World Evangelism has called Christians around the world to fast after the style of John Wesley: to take no food after lunch on Thursday until mid-afternoon (supper) on Friday. Not only does such a practice help us keep perspective on our conspicuous consumption, not only does it sensitize us to the needs of others, especially the millions that are dying of starvation, it gives us an opportunity to enter into solidarity with Christians around the world in praying for revival and the coming of God's reign of righteousness, justice, and peace.

Reflecting and Recording

Spend a bit of time reflecting on the place fasting has in your life. Do you fast? What does it mean to you? Why don't you fast?

■ ■ ■

Spend some time reflecting on this dimension of fasting: denying ourselves food as an act of remembering. Reread the paragraph about remembering on page 175.

■ ■ ■

The prophet Isaiah described the fast in this way:

- to loose the bonds of injustice,
- to undo the thongs of the yoke,
- to let the oppressed go free,
- to share bread with the hungry,
- to provide housing for the poor,
- to clothe the naked.

Look at the list. Have you "fasted" in any of these ways during the past three months? Check the ones that you have practiced.

■ ■ ■

Close your time considering what decision you should make about fasting. Are you inspired to try it? Will you experiment with it for three months? Give this prayerful consideration.

During the Day

If you haven't finished making arrangements for a "special meal" with someone, do so today. Find out if there is a group in your church that is practicing fasting in a disciplined way. Is this something you would like to talk to your pastor about?

DAY 7

Evil Desires Nailed to the Cross

Well then, shall we keep on sinning so that God can keep on showing us more and more kindness and forgiveness? Of course not! Should we keep on sinning when we don't have to? For sin's power over us was broken when we became Christians and were baptized to become a part of Jesus Christ; through his death the power of your sinful nature was shattered. Your old sin-loving nature was buried with him by baptism when he died, and when God the Father, with glorious power, brought him back to life again, you were given his wonderful new life to enjoy.

For you have become a part of him, and so you died with him, so to speak, when he died; and now you share his new life, and shall rise as he did. Your old evil desires were nailed to the cross with him; that part of you that loves to sin was crushed and fatally wounded, so that your sin-loving body is no longer under sin's control, no longer needs to be a slave to sin; for when you are deadened to sin you are freed from all its allure and its power over you.

—Romans 6:1-7, *The Living Bible* paraphrase

The word of Paul to the Romans is promising and powerful. The images are strong and vivid: the power of your sinful nature was shattered; your old sin-loving nature was buried with him by baptism; that part of you that loves to sin was crushed and fatally wounded; your sin-loving body is no longer under sin's control.

The Christian is a *new person*: baptized to become a part of Jesus Christ; given Jesus' wonderful life to enjoy, we now share Christ's new life; freed from sin's allure and its power over us.

This is the last day of this workbook journey, and we need to claim the promise and power life in Christ offers. We do not have to be victims of sin's power. Even after we become Christians, sin remains in our life, but no longer does it reign. As Paul said, we are to look upon our old sinful nature as dead and unresponsive to sin, and instead be alive or alert to God, through Jesus Christ our Lord. (See Romans 6:11.)

We gain a saving perspective on these radical claims when we ask the right question. Our usual response to the question as to whether a Christian sins is "Of course!" But the more important question is whether a Christian has to sin. The answer to that is a resounding no!

Sin is a conquered foe. "For this purpose the Son of God was manifested, that He might destroy the works of the devil" (1 John 3:8, NKJV). "You know that He was manifested to take away our sins; and in Him there is no sin" (1 John 3:5, NKJV). The witness of scripture is clear: Sin is a conquered foe. We can share in that victory.

Here is the key: In any given situation, God's grace is more powerful than the lure of temptation. That's where we must begin. That's the bedrock truth, and it is the witness of scripture over and over again. It is also one of the strongest tenets in John Wesley's theology: Regenerative and sanctifying grace keeps us so long as we keep it.

There is a sense in which we will always struggle with some facet of sin seeking control of some part of our life. The call upon us is to surrender ourselves entirely to the will of God. Surrender is more important than struggle. To be sure, we live in daily self-examination, watchful for every effort evil makes to get a foothold in our life. We fight back!

But all of our fighting will be for naught if we are not yielded to God's will. Our human resources are not adequate for the war that goes on inside us; nor will we have the strength to withstand the allure of envy and lust and greed and gluttony. So "look upon your old sinful nature as dead." We keep that vision a reality through ongoing surrender of our will to Christ. Surrendered to Christ, the reality of his pardon and the power of his presence make real in our attitudes and practices what we claim in our hearts and minds.

Yesterday we considered fasting as an antidote for gluttony. Fasting will mean all Christ intends only when accompanied by surrender. The outward act of fasting will do us some good, but it will not release power and bring transformation unless it serves as a token of our self-offering. Fasting must be more than self-denial; it must be the outward and visible sign of our being completely available to God.

This is the only weapon that will enable us to win the battle with the seven deadly sins: an unquestioned acceptance of God's grace and pardon, and a complete surrender to God.

Reflecting and Recording

Take a long look at yourself as you think about sin and grace, your struggle with sin, the degree to which you feel guilty, whether you have fully accepted the forgiveness Christ offers, and the level of your surrender to him. Allow these thoughts to guide you in a few minutes of reflection.

■ ■ ■

Focus your reflection now by answering this question: If God could tell you one thing about himself, and only one, what do you imagine it would be? Write the word here.

Now this: If God could make one request of you, and only one, what do you imagine it would be? Write that request here.

Close your time in prayer, thanking God for the insights and learnings given to you during this workbook adventure and renewing whatever commitments you are being called to make.

And every day, from now on, remember that your only effective weapon against sin is surrender. When you surrender you can sing

> Perfect submission, all is at rest;
> I in my Savior am happy and blest.

Group Meeting for Week Eight

Note: The leader for this week should bring a whiteboard or newsprint to the meeting. See number 4 of Sharing Together.

Introduction

This is the last meeting designed for this group. You have already talked about the possibility of continuing to meet. You should conclude those plans.

Whatever you choose to do, it is usually helpful to determine the actual time line in order that persons can make a clear commitment. Assign some persons to follow through with whatever decisions are made.

Sharing Together

Your sharing during this session should reflect on the entire eight-week experience. (Leader: save enough time to respond to suggestions 10 and 11.) Begin with your workbook experience this past week.

1. Let each person share any new insight or learning that came this week.
2. Spend four to six minutes talking about the relationship between gluttony and lust.
3. If it is true that we can be gluttonous with shopping, work, alcohol, tobacco, soap operas, gambling, exercise, video games, etc., go around the circle with each person repeating this sentence, filling in the blank: "If I am guilty of gluttony, I am gluttonous with _____."
4. Take this sharing a bit further. Have a scribe record on the whiteboard or newsprint as people share. Turn to your Reflecting and Recording section of Day 2. As you are willing, name aloud the areas of your life where you are tempted to overindulge. The scribe should record each different one, putting an X beside any one as it is repeated. This will give you a picture of the things in which we overindulge, but also our most common overindulgences.
5. Look at the recorded listing and spend ten to fifteen minutes discussing our "sin of consumerism" and our effort to feed the soul with the body's food.

6. Spend six to eight minutes discussing the claim: "We buy and consume to fill our emptiness and to give us a sense of worth."

7. Invite at least two persons to share the prayer they wrote during their Reflecting and Recording on Day 3.

8. As we considered during Week Seven, Paul said our bodies are to be a "temple of the Holy Spirit." Saint Francis of Assisi referred to his body as "Brother Ass." Talk for a few minutes about the likenesses and differences of these images.

9. Spend eight to ten minutes discussing how fasting and feasting should be incorporated in your life and the life of the congregation. Share any personal experiences of fasting and also any experiences of "special meals" you may have had this week.

10. Take twelve to eighteen minutes with persons sharing what this eight weeks has meant to them—new insights, challenges, things they will have to work on.

11. Spend the balance of your time discussing the answer to all sin: our surrender to God and our willingness to yield our wills to him.

Praying Together

1. Invite each person to share a commitment he/she has made, a confession of a particular sin, a specific temptation, an ongoing struggle—any concern about which he/she wishes the group to pray. As each person shares, have a time of prayer—silent or verbal, hopefully verbal—so that each person will be specifically prayed for.

2. Now invite two or three persons to offer general prayers of thanksgiving for the eight-week experience and petitions for further growth and guidance.

3. A benediction is a blessing or greeting shared with another or by a group in parting. A variation on the traditional "passing of the peace" can serve as a benediction. Take a person's hand, look into his or her eyes, and say, "The peace of God be with you," and the person responds, "And may God's peace be yours." Then that person takes the hand of the person next to him or her and says, "The peace of God be with you," and receives the response, "And may God's peace be yours." Standing in a circle, let the leader "pass the peace," and let it go around the circle.

4. Having completed the passing of the peace, speak to one another in a more spontaneous way. Move about to different persons in the group, saying whatever you feel is appropriate for your parting blessing to each person. Or you may simply embrace the person and say nothing. In your own unique way, "bless" each person who has shared this journey with you.

BIBLIOGRAPHY

Abbott, Dorothy, ed. *Mississippi Writers: Reflections of Childhood and Youth, Volume 1: Fiction.* University of Mississippi, 1985

Blanding, Don. *Joy Is an Inside Job.* New York: Dodd, Mead & Company, 1953.

Buechner, Frederick. *Wishful Thinking: A Theological ABC.* New York: Harper & Row, 1973.

Campolo, Anthony. *Seven Deadly Sins.* Wheaton, IL: Victor Books, 1987.

Dostoyevsky, Fyodor. *The Brothers Karamazov.* New York: Random House, Inc., 1950.

Fairlie, Henry. *The Seven Deadly Sins Today.* Washington, D.C.: New Republic Books, 1978.

Graham, Billy. *The 7 Deadly Sins.* Grand Rapids, MI: Zondervan Publishing House, 1955.

Holloway, Richard. *Seven to Flee, Seven to Follow.* London: Mowbray, 1986.

Keen, Sam. *Inward Bound: Exploring the Geography of Your Emotions.* New York: Bantam Books, 1980.

Larsen, Earnie, and Carol Hegarty. *Believing in Myself: Daily Meditations for Healing and Building Self-Esteem.* New York: Prentice Hall Press, 1991.

Llewelyn, Robert, introduced and arranged. *The Joy of the Saints: Spiritual Readings throughout the Year.* Springfield, IL.: Templegate Publishers, 1989

Maclaren, Alexander. *Expositions of Holy Scripture.* Amazon Digital Services LLC, 2012.

McCracken, Robert J. *What Is Sin? What Is Virtue?* New York: Harper & Row, 1966.

Olsson, Karl A. *Seven Sins and Seven Virtues.* New York: Harper and Brothers, 1959.

Sayers, Dorothy L. *The Other Six Deadly Sins.* London: Methuen & Co. LTD., 1943.

Schimmel, Solomon. *The Seven Deadly Sins: Jewish, Christian, and Classical Reflections on Human Nature.* New York: The Free Press, 1992.

Shoemaker, H. Stephen. *The Jekyll and Hyde Syndrome: A New Encounter with the Seven Deadly Sins and Seven Lively Virtues.* Nashville, TN: Broadman Press, 1987.

Stalker, James. *The Seven Deadly Sins.* London: Hodder & Stoughton, 1901.

The Works of John Wesley: Volume V. Grand Rapids: Zondervan Publishing House, 1872.

Webb, Lance. *Conquering the Seven Deadly Sins.* Nashville, TN: Abingdon, 1955.

———. *How Good Are Your Virtues? The Transforming Power of Love.* Nashville, TN: Abingdon Press, 1959.

White, William R. *Fatal Attraction: Sermons on the Seven Deadly Sins.* Nashville, TN: Abingdon Press, 1959.

Whitlow, Brian. *Hurdles to Heaven.* New York: Harper & Row, 1963.

AFFIRMATION CARDS

Pride goes before destruction, and a haughty spirit before a fall.

—Proverbs 16:18

I Am a Unique, Unrepeatable Miracle of God.

The Lord Jesus Christ "will change our weak mortal bodies and make them like his own glorious body, using that power by which he is able to bring all things under his rule."

—Philippians 3:21, GNT

O Lord, make me an instrument of your peace.
Where there is hatred let me sow love;
Where there is injury, pardon;
Where there is doubt, faith;
Where there is despair, hope;
Where there is darkness, light;
Where there is sadness, joy.

—Attributed to Saint Francis of Assisi

CPSIA information can be obtained at www.ICGtesting.com
Printed in the USA
LVOW09s1911201016

509632LV00006B/15/P